BULLET PROOF

PROOF

B R A N D I N G

CHRIS WESTFALL

BulletProof Branding

© 2014 By

Chris Westfall

ALL RIGHTS RESERVED

Foreword by Ted Rubin

Cover design by Brenda Phelps Shih

ISBN: 978-0-9854148-2-5

First Printing: 2014

MARIE STREET PRESS
5760 Legacy Drive
Suite B3-454
Plano, TX 75024

Tel +1 214.519.8033

http://bulletproofbranding.info

http://mariestreetpress.com

To Bill Moncrief and Chuck Lamb

Because that's where this conversation got started

"Delivering an amazing experience for your customer starts with an amazing brand. Today, branding impacts every aspect of the customer-focused business. Read this book and create the focus you need, for your brand."

Shep Hyken,
customer service expert and
New York Times bestselling author

"Brand equity is not just for companies to build and protect – it's personal and it's for each one of us. Chris' book will show you how to create, manage and maintain a powerful brand for yourself. Important stuff!"

Dennis McTighe,
Vice President, Sales -National Accounts, LG Electronics

"A significant key for growing your business is the ability to differentiate yourself from the competition. Chris Westfall shows entrepreneurs and business owners an easy to implement system for engaging clients & customers. Regardless of the size of your organization, I definitely recommend you read this book."

Mark Satterfield,
CEO and Founder, Gentle Rain Marketing Inc.

"Confident and straightforward, Chris' guidance has helped me and our clients tremendously. Definitely the guy to go to for anything related to B2B communications in today's marketplace!"

Summer Coley-Ward,

Marketing Strategist, Agent Noir Marketing Group Inc.

"Social selling is vital to your business. But without a great brand, you've got nothing. This book is changing the conversation - read it and find out what your brand has been missing."

Kurt Shaver,

LinkedIn Expert and CEO, The Sales Foundry

Table of Contents

Foreword

WHAT IS YOUR RELATIONSHIP with your brand?

Getting the right message to the right people at the right time is an age-old marketing mantra. And how you hit that sweet spot has been foremost in the minds of every marketer since people started selling things to each other. That hasn't changed over the years, but our ability to connect with each other and gather information about each other has.

Today, technology brings us closer together as people. However, as marketers we have to look at new technologies not as solutions, but as tools for driving conversation. We need to be more focused on personal connection and on using technology to build and nurture relationships.

That's why I wrote *Return on Relationship* with Kathryn Rose – because the concept of personal connection is one that transcends time and technology. In this book, Chris Westfall has created a different kind of roadmap to the branding conversation – a conversation that considers the people that matter most to your brand. More importantly, he offers insight into what companies like Cisco, IBM and Cargill are doing to further the conversation – a conversation that's enabled by technology, but strategically determined by people. People just like you.

The bottom line is really your mindset and how you approach marketing in the first place. Are you in it for the most part to get more eyeballs, or are you in it to develop relationships? The conversation around your brands' value is a two-way dialogue, and you owe it to yourself to consider the strategies included in this book. It doesn't matter if you are the social media manager for a multi-billion dollar brand or a solopreneur interested in better personal branding. The concepts you need to build the relationships you deserve are all here for you.

As you begin this book, consider these questions about your organization:

- What is the story around your products and services?
- Who is telling that story... and from whose perspective?
- Are you building relationships that lead to greater advocacy, more true fans, and clear and measurable results for your business?

- Do you have a strategy in place to make sure your message is consistent – not just in your marketing department, but from the C-Suite to customer service to the shop floor?
- Are you sure your message is authentic (no matter who tells your story)?

If you're trying to make decisions right now about how to improve your brand, then these are just a few of the questions you need to ask yourself. The relationships you cultivate will determine the value of your business.

If you're reading this book, you're interested in making those relationships matter and turning connections into clear profitability. Take the journey and find out what Chris has discovered via his own experience, as well as the relevant interviews that he's compiled for you.

There are a lot of ideas out there about what marketing and branding really means. However, you'll make the right decisions as long as improved relationships (which lead to trust, loyalty and advocacy) are your major goals. That's what I call a real Return on Relationship—and building strong relationships starts with your story. Chris Westfall's take on the new context for your brand is a story that can, if you allow it, create a transformation in the way you approach the people that matter most.

- TED RUBIN

Introduction: When Brands Are Broken

THE SYSTEM WAS HACKED in 2008. March 31, 2008, to be exact. That's the day that everything went offline, then online again, eventually. But after this date, nothing was ever going to be the same.

People had been trying for years to break in, blow it up, change the game. Others say the change happened elsewhere, on another day or in another place. But on this day, in Chicago, everything transformed. The power shifted.

One of the largest and most respected brands in the US was going to be brought to its knees. Through a series of missteps, the power was going to shift. Branding was going to change. And there was suddenly a new sheriff in town, laying down some unlikely laws about what branding really means.

On March 31, 2008, the marketing mix suddenly became wild. Uncontrolled. Vulnerable.

The crack in the system was too big to ignore, and yet - when the corporation did ignore it - the result was game-changing, and irreversible.

At the center of the story was the hacker, the one who would take back the power.

A cataclysmic branding shift was set in motion by none other than a soft-spoken Canadian country singer.

Flying from Halifax to Omaha on United Airlines, musician Dave Carroll and his band, Sons of Maxwell, had a layover in Chicago.

Waiting patiently on the tarmac, he overheard a nearby passenger gasp, and then cry out, "Oh my God!"

Dave turned to look at what was going on outside the window.

That's when he saw it. "They're throwing... guitars!" said a voice in the cabin.

Carroll watched in terror as his $3,500 Taylor guitar flew through the friendly skies... and landed on the unforgiving tarmac.

Upon arrival in Omaha, Taylor discovered what you probably already suspect. The neck of his guitar had been broken.

He complained to United. Repeatedly. They didn't listen.

And a yearlong journey of customer service missteps exposed a gaping hole in the airline's branding. The whole idea of "customer service" became twisted into a horrible nightmare.

Yet Carroll remained calm in seeking some sort of compensation, even suggesting a $1200 flight voucher to settle the matter.

That's right. The damage to his guitar was just $1200.

The answer to every request was a simple and curt, "No."

No voucher.
No repair.
No liability.
No thank you.

The airline referred him back to Halifax, then to Air Canada, then to New York, and back to Chicago, as they repeatedly rejected and denied his claim.

Quietly, this endless customer service disaster was providing Carroll with the ammunition he needed. He was going to change the conversation with United.

And he did.

His YouTube video, "United Breaks Guitars," became an instant sensation in 2009, with over 3 million hits in its first week. United's branding blow-up launched a speaking and writing career for Carroll (his book is called - wait for it - *United Breaks Guitars*). You can view the entire story on his website, http://davecarrollmusic.com or visit the customer-centric site he helped co-found, http://gripevine.com. As this is being written, the "United" video has over 13 million views.

It's easy to see Dave's story as simply a customer service issue. Characters in the plot include flight attendants, customer service personnel, and various others within the marketing machine of the airline. But one person emerged as the hero of the story. The hero was Dave Carroll.

For United, it was an expensive lesson in how not to handle a simple complaint: by some estimates, the popularity of Carroll's YouTube video cost the airline approximately 10% in stock value - about $180 million.[1]

In four minutes, the viral video pierced the armor-plated branding of the largest airline in the world. And the irony is, United gave him all the ammunition he could possibly need.

Think about that for a second: what could you or another employee do to create a $180 million dollar swing in a publicly traded company? What action could you take that would have similar impact?

Before you pick up an (unbroken) guitar and start busting out some new lyrics on YouTube, consider the real shift that was created with Carroll's song and story.

Carroll had completely hacked the system.

In Halifax, he was just a passenger. Just like you. Just like me. He was just a customer.

Then he arrived in Chicago. From there, he changed the value of the entire airline.

The singer from Nova Scotia was given the power to create change in powerful and unprecedented ways. United Airlines - the world's largest airline, with over 86,000 employees - was forced to face the music.

The Big Brand wasn't bulletproof.

Control of United's brand wasn't in the hands of the marketing department, or the PR spokesperson, or their advertising agency, or any member of the executive staff.

The customer took control of the conversation.

And the Big Brand had to listen.

Carroll's story is not just about poor customer service, it's about the nature of branding in the new economy. The Suggestion Box has been replaced with Pandora's Box - a constant stream of Everyman reporters, all armed with cameras (and some with guitars), with the ability to document and influence change in 140 characters or less.

While social media has provided a new voice to many, Carroll's story cracked the code in a way that redefined what branding means.

In this book, you'll learn what you've got to know about branding in the modern age. What is the new code, exactly, for the branding conversation? Who controls it?

How can you influence your branding - online, in person and in print? The balance of power has shifted - so, what are the risks to you and your brand?

Clearly, the customer's role has changed - that means your role has shifted as well. Doesn't matter if you are a CMO at a multinational corporation, or a sophomore at Colorado State building a LinkedIn profile. You are a brand, and you represent a brand.

Your branding is either good or bad, there's no in-between.

There's no "opt out" of branding.

Either you're bulletproof, or you're not.

So, let's focus on what you need to know to make this shift work for you.

In order to set the stage for the discussion of your branding, it's important to redefine some important terms.

First of all, the idea of branding. What does branding mean to you?

As Jeffrey Hayzlett famously shared in *The Mirror Test*, branding was something originally done to cattle - as a sign of ownership. Brands differentiated bovines, separating one herd from the next. In a business context, branding came to be an important part of an overall marketing mix.

Branding is a very powerful thing, indeed.

The branding of the New York Yankees has created the most valuable sports franchise in the USA.[2] With $330 million in revenues in 2012, the team is currently valued at over $2.3 Billion. There's power in the pinstripes, and evidently winning isn't everything (said the Texas Rangers fan, with a wry smile). But there's no stopping the branding power behind the Yankees.

Branding survives the scandals and the losses, and goes beyond the stadium, the players and even the fans.

Branding is about value - the value of the organization.

If you want to create maximum value - and that includes maximum revenues - you've got to have a bulletproof brand.

Because branding is the number one way to create value for yourself and for your organization.

In fact, branding impacts every facet of your company.

Did you think that branding was just a function of marketing? Au contraire, mon frère.

If the marketing department creates a fantastic package and an online campaign to match it, plus traditional print advertising backed by an exciting website/microsite campaign but the execution is disappointing, guess what? Operations, shipping, distribution and every level of executive management just created a branding failure.

Of epic proportions.

But don't take my word for it. Just check the YouTube videos, blogs, twitter feeds and 362 other online sources that mention the disappointment in your branding.

Branding isn't about broadcasting. Branding is the very essence of your organization, and everyone in the company plays a role.

So, if you're wondering if bulletproof branding requires:

- Great customer service
- Expert sales strategies
- World-class operational excellence
- Impeccable logistics and delivery
- Intelligent distribution
- Worldwide consistency
- Laser-focused leadership
- Confirmation from your customers

The answer to all of the above is: Yes.

Leave out any one part of excellence and excellence ceases to exist.

In other words: one misstep, and your branding isn't bulletproof. No amount of promotion or public relations trickery can cover for operational or strategic malfunction.

Branding is not a function within the organization. **Branding *is* the organization.**

Your brand is not a billboard, or a package, or a logo. Not anymore.

Sure, presentation is a part of the overall package. But a great design with lousy service is a branding disaster.

The facade will fade quickly under the harsh glare of social media, instant communication, and re-imagined reputations.

- No sexy image can overcome the impact of a broken guitar.
- Poorly engineered products that fail to deliver are a branding nightmare.
- "We suck less than the competition" is not really a strategy. Ever work for a company like that?

So, what exactly is the definition of branding in the new economy?

It has been said, by Hayzlett and others, that a brand is a promise delivered.

My question is: who decides when it's delivered?

In a PC-world (that's "post-Carroll"), branding is more than just a promise. Because brands make promises, real or implied, all the time.

Consider these "branding" moves by Chipotle on Twitter. In July of 2013, a series of bizarre messages were sent out – sparking publicity and making it appear that the Chipotle Twitter account had been hacked. The messages were repeated – many of the tweets made no sense – but, when they were not deleted, people started to wonder: what's really going on?

Amidst the flurry of 140-character blasts, the brand revealed its "Great Burrito Hack" was a hoax. The broadcast messages were a lie.

"The aim was to spark conversation," according to Chris Arnold, Chipotle's unapologetic Communications Director. Typically, Arnold explained, the company adds about 250 followers a day. But, look at these numbers: Chipotle gained 4,000 new followers as a result of the stunt.[3]

Was the "Burrito Hack" a win? Was the strategy bulletproof?

Any strategy that creates inconsistency and mistrust isn't bulletproof. Shenanigans and stunts are called "gimmicks." According to their website (here's the link http://www.chipotle.com/en-us/fwi/fwi.aspx), Chipotle is a company that prides itself on integrity. And if something backfires, you're not bulletproof.

All publicity isn't good publicity. Making noise is not the same as making money. In fact, sometimes it's the exact opposite.

What does a stunt say about your publicity, and about the brand?

With multiple 24-hour news media outlets, there's a desperate need for constant content. Stories - whether newsworthy or not - are cluttering the airwaves.

A branding strategy can help you to contribute to the chatter.

Bulletproof branding cuts through the noise.

What kind of message do you want to convey about your brand?

Please phrase your answer in the form of a customer.

___

What's on, on your website? One of the most powerful tools for creating the branding conversation is a video. That's one of the key takeaways from the story of Dave Carroll.

As a means of summary at the end of each chapter, I'll provide you with some key insights that you can turn into actionable steps for your brand. Let's start your story with a quick message about how to utilize video to make your story stronger and the conversation more compelling.

The first question for you is: *Do you have a YouTube channel?*

More than one billion unique visitors visit YouTube each month, as of this writing. And that number is only going to increase. Consider these additional statistics:

- YouTube reaches more US adults age 18-34 than any cable network (notice the wording: not any cable channel, any cable network)[4]
- Mobile devices now make up almost 40% of YouTube's global watch time[4] (that's as I write - wonder what that number is now, as you read this?)

Not only are YouTube videos a source of revenue (according to Google, "thousands" of channels are earning six figures a year from video production[4]) but as the number two search engine, it pays to have a strong presence in the medium.

The Business Insider, in an article entitled "TV Is Dying, And Here Are The Stats That Prove It" from November 2013, shares these statistics[5]:

- Since 2010, approximately five million people ended their cable and broadband subscriptions (presumably turning to free access points, like Starbucks, across the US for internet access)
- Cable television prices are increasing in order to meet revenue targets with an ever-shrinking audience. Result? Television advertising isn't reaching the masses. It's reaching a semi-elite audience that can still afford to subscribe to cable – and an audience that, for whatever reason, hasn't figured out how to access programs and entertainment via more cost-effective means. Does that describe your target market? There's no right or wrong answer – only incorrect segmentation. You want to make sure your medium fits your message – and your audience – if your brand is going to be bulletproof.
- In November of 2013, TV still stands as the most prevalent mass medium in the US, reaching 294 million Americans (according to Business Insider).[6]   But Facebook has 200 million viewers. Google says they've got 235 million. And the online mass media message is going to overtake TV – maybe it already has, depending on when you are reading this book!

- According to Cisco research from 2013, featured in Business Insider, mobile video traffic is set to increase nearly 500% by 2016. In raw numbers, consumption is predicted to leap from less than one million TB per month (that's terabytes) to roughly six million terabytes per month, worldwide.

The bottom line? People in the US (and around the globe) are spending more time with digital media. In the UK, online usage is increasing in similar fashion, according to this article in The Guardian, with the headline, "Britons spend one in 12 waking minutes online…" As a result, video advertising grew 86%, online display advertising grew 23% and mobile search advertising jumped 101%.[7]

There's no doubt that TV watching is declining and the proliferation of tablets and mobile devices means more to your brand than ever.

For larger organizations, access to production facilities and strategic use of YouTube is blended into the marketing mix – a mix that typically includes traditional television advertising, for larger consumer-focused brands. And every savvy marketer will tell you that Super Bowl advertising is the best way to present your message to 100 million eyeballs across a three-hour time frame.

But bulletproof branding is more targeted than a mass media blitz. And you don't need $4 million to be bulletproof (that's the average cost of a 30-second spot for the 2014 Super Bowl).[8] YouTube is not only the great budgetary equalizer: the opportunity to segment, target and communicate directly with your customer has created an unbelievable video opportunity for you.

TIGHTEN THE STORY

The best way to connect with your audience and to create a bulletproof conversation is via an effective online video strategy. For many companies, bloggers and individual brands, the story begins in video.

So, are you ready for your close-up? Here are three simple video ideas that you can implement, right now, whether you are a solopreneur or internationally recognized brand:

1. Begin the conversation with what others are saying: Do you have a good testimonial video? What do your best customers know and appreciate about you? Providing that information is much more effective than advertising when it comes to connecting to your brand.

2. Stop investing so much in television advertising: the conversation is online. Your branding message is being viewed online.

3. The camera never lies: back off of the big-time production values if you want your conversation to resonate. While quality is important (your video has to be watchable if you want people to watch it), over-produced videos read as sales-y and fake. Show real people gaining real advantages from your solution – not CGI-injected modeltastic folks receiving some sort of alternative-reality mind-blast that rivals the visuals from Avatar. Unless that's an effective description of your product, your market and your intended budget – featuring James Cameron at the helm of your YouTube channel, of course.

Chapter 1: Redefining Your Brand

Nothing is too difficult. You only need to know how.
YIDDISH PROVERB

*It is far more impressive when others discover your
good qualities without your help.*
JUDITH MARTIN (MISS MANNERS)

BRANDING HAS MANY COMPONENTS. Branding is about a promise delivered, as Jeffrey Hayzlett talks about in *The Mirror Test*. On a simpler level, you could say that branding is what others say about you.

In other words, branding is your reputation.

And a brand is also the representation of your product or service.

Yet, none of those definitions is really comprehensive enough, in my opinion. There needs to be an understanding of branding that's bulletproof – an understanding that touches every aspect of your organization. Including your customers and prospects.

And, that definition should be simple – clear – and powerful enough to inspire the corner office as well as the customer service team, while reaching the folks in engineering and accounting as well.

Branding is really about *exchange*.

The exchange of ideas. The exchange of new strategies. The exchange of solutions. The exchange of images and products and tweets and comments and services and more. All designed to create the ultimate exchange: the exchange of your brand, for revenues.

Bulletproof branding creates that exchange consistently, carefully and deliberately across all aspects of your organization.

Bulletproof branding helps your organization to create exchange.

The exchange of ideas online is part of your branding. The exchange of money for goods and services is also about branding, so sales and marketing are all under the same circus tent. (Let's see if any fights break out. Keep your eye on the clown car).

And branding is also about execution - bringing promises to life in a way that is recognized at the highest levels of your organization.

No, not the executive suite. The highest level is reserved for your most important person. That would be: the customer.

In this book, we'll talk about new ways to create exchange. Branding is about reaching customers in new and more meaningful ways, and then helping your customers to reach more customers. That's a plan that's bulletproof, if (and it's a big "if") you know how to pull it off.

To learn more about the process, I've included insights from companies both large and small – branding strategies that have propelled organizations forward in the new economy. These stories will show you the "how" of creating a more powerful brand message – and guiding the conversation that helps others to know how great you are (without broadcasting, bulldozing or barraging your audience).

Remember, the balance of power has shifted, and the customer now rules supreme as the Chief Branding Officer.

Creating the exchange you want, and your customers deserve, requires six fundamental principles. Six pillars, if you will, of *BulletProof Branding*. These six pillars apply whether you are branding a person, product or idea. These principles apply online, as well as face-to-face.

After all, that's what principles are - like the law of gravity, they always work. Doesn't matter if you're in Australia, Antwerp or Abilene.

And principles never have the stigma of "Because I said so" or some implied expertise.

As you read about these six pillars, you and you alone will be the expert on your brand.

My job is simply to provide a new way of looking at the same old problems (and a few new ones). The coming chapters will address these six principles in detail, but here they are in brief:

- **Consistency** - making your URL match up with IRL (in real life)
- **Clarity** - your story and your theme. What's your "Big Idea?"

- **Collaboration** - Why branding is a team sport. And how to play the game.
- **Context** - the wind-up determines the pitch. Here's why.
- **Capitalizing** - turning your branding into an asset. Leveraging what you've built.
- **Craving** - Keep 'em wanting more. Teasers, tokens and follow-through.

Within the text, you will see examples of brands that are changing the conversation and changing their results. But more than just an overview of branding (haven't we all read a book about how great Apple is?) or an academic textbook, the aim of *BulletProof Branding* is action.

Each of the chapters will include action steps as part of a summary, so that you can put new ideas into your brand.

The goal is to show you, through these six principles, what you can do today to transform your marketing – no, wait a minute. Make that, "your organization." Whether you represent a person, product or idea, the key to your results begins with the conversation.

Understanding how to create the conversation, to provide influence, and ultimately, how to turn your customers into branding advocates, is our path.

That's the kind of exchange that's truly bulletproof.

Along the way, you will see exercises and ideas that can make a difference: whether you are your own brand, or you own a multi-national brand, you'll find a new look at marketing inside these pages. More importantly, you'll understand how to protect and strengthen your branding, based on expert perspectives and proven techniques for making your message matter.

It's time to recognize and capitalize on the fundamental shift that Dave Carroll showed us.

The customer is King. And the conversation rules the realm.

Chapter 2: Consistency

For me, the challenge isn't to be different but to be consistent.

JOAN JETT

DOES YOUR URL MATCH UP with IRL?

(That's IRL, "in real life.")

Consistency is a key component of effective branding. If people meet you in person, and you don't live up to your avatar, well, you've got a problem.

Similarly, if you're Doubletree Hotels (where the "little things mean everything") and the cookies in the lobby are stale, the maid doesn't service that room before 5:00pm and the front desk clerk dismisses a guest's concerns...well, those little things add up to one big thing: namely, that your brand is inconsistent. (Luckily, Doubletree seems to be one of the most consistent of all hotel brands).

But inconsistent really means "disappointing," in the context of branding.

Beyond dissatisfaction, the conversation around your brand now focuses on inconsistency.

Suddenly, your Chief Branding Officer is focused on what's out of sync.

Wait a minute: you don't know who your Chief Branding Officer is? Well, your CBO is more important than your CEO, or any other member of the C-Suite. The CBO isn't always right, but the CBO is always the CBO.

The Chief Branding Officer is now the customer.

If customer is an uncomfortable term, think of "your audience." Your followers and friends are serving as your Chief Branding Officer.

Your Chief Branding Officer controls your brand. Bulletproof branding is about influencing and guiding the CBO.

So what influences the CBO?

Consistency.

After all, it's not what you say about your brand that counts. It's what others say.

So the post is not as important as the share.

The comments matter more than the pictures.

The brand is found in the conversation. Is that story consistent? Is your message persuasive? Is that persuasion conveyed by people *who are not on your payroll*?

You can influence your brand, but the Chief Branding Officer is the one who ultimately establishes its value. The CBO knows about the transfer of power: a transfer from the business brand to the customer's voice.

Branding is not broadcasting. The conversation about your brand goes both ways.

Bulletproof branding is a conversation.

Creating slogans is a relatively simple task, requiring some cleverness. It can be as simple as a change in a website or in an online profile. The responses, likes and shares are where the artistry comes into play.

How does your message measure up? Are you clever, or consistent? You better be both, if you want to be remembered.

Without cleverness, your message is old news and lost in the noise. No one is listening if you can't create a story around your brand that is:

- innovative
- surprising
- counter-intuitive
- unexpected

Without one of these four elements, your audience says, "So what?"

Your message has added noise, but no real resonance. No one is going to get your story. Or, even worse: retweet you.

How do you create an authentic message?

If consistency is your goal, you've got to find your way to that clear, concise and compelling story behind your brand.

Who decides if your story is authentic?

Consider this scenario:

In the game of "Three Truths and a Lie," you deliver three stories that are true, and one is false. You share all stories with the same level of skill, and (if you play the game to win) the same level of detachment, so that your body language and tone of voice don't betray you.

But one of the stories is false.

One story is not authentic.

One story is not consistent with the truth.

Who decides which one is authentic?

You know your story. Maybe you've even considered how to tell it, and so you can craft a "believable" message - even for a story that's false.

But authenticity, like beauty, is in the eye of the beholder.

Therefore, if you want to create a consistent message, consider the source of your consistency.

It ain't you. It's your audience.
Consistently.

Without consistency, your customers are confused and disappointed. Would your audience say that your brand is consistent? If they don't, it isn't.

Branding isn't just a one-way exercise, where you say who you are and what you do. That's yesterday's news.

Without consistency, your branding is an empty promise. Without delivery and execution, your clients will be left wondering why you are overpaying your marketing department. Or maybe that you need to hire a marketing department.

All around you are signs of inconsistency for the brands you have come to know and trust. And some of those "brands" are institutions, offering a promise that is rarely delivered.

Examples include your favorite church, or your state government, or national sports figures. Ever been disappointed by a real or implied promise, that somehow went South?

Without consistency, you engender mistrust. For both genders, of course.

Without trust, you jeopardize the one thing that's already in short supply: brand loyalty. How can clients be loyal to something (or someone) they can't trust?

Trust comes from predictability. You know exactly what you can expect when you see those Golden Arches, or that green logo on the Starbucks sign.

But what's the story for the unestablished brand? How can a person or a company create a sense of trust and consistency, when the story is new, the track record unestablished, and the brand promise undefined?

Consistency Starts with Your Story

The greatest brands of all time, from Ford to Apple and everything in between, all began at the same starting point. The clothes you wear, the car you drive, the house you live in all started in the exact same place as well.

Someone said, "I have an idea." Maybe that someone was Henry Ford. Or Steve Jobs. Or your future husband.

And someone else said, "Tell me more."

The conversation is a powerful tool.

Consistency implies a series of similar events, behaviors or outcomes.

Consistency creates trust. And consistency requires the engagement and support of every division within the organization. Marketing can't "go it alone," or build an entire campaign that isn't reflective of the entire organization.

Predictability drives consumer behavior, as well as business partnerships. Starting place for all of the above? A conversation.

Your ability to influence the consistency of your brand happens on a daily basis, within every phase of your operation. The first step starts with you. Your message must be clear, and your operational execution begins the story at a level that goes beyond words.

A Personal Branding Exercise: Tell Me More... About the Brand Called "You."

Ok, so branding doesn't begin with your advertising agency, or your social media campaign.

And, if you're a solopreneur or small business, you don't even have a "campaign." Or, do you?

Before you send that next tweet, think about how you are a part of your branding message.

Products and services are brands, but so are you. In fact, branding begins with you - your story, expressed in a way that's authentic and compelling.

So... Is your story authentic and compelling?

Be careful with your answer.

Guess who decides if you are authentic or not?

(Nope, it's not me.)

It's the same person that decides on "compelling."

There's only one person who can decide that your message is authentic and compelling:

It's your audience.

Think about the tools you use to tell your story: your website, your Twitter account, your company collateral, or even your resume.

The reaction you receive depends on your branding.

Personal branding really depends on your ability to create exchange: an exchange of ideas, an exchange of words... or even: an exchange of your talents that results in a paycheck.

The principle behind personal branding is "Tell me More..."

And, since bulletproof branding is a dialogue, we'll shift from a broadcast branding model to the one thing that every brand needs and requires in the digital economy:

Influence.

The influential conversation begins with the customer, of course. But the real question is: what kind of message do you want *your customer* to convey about your brand?

That's the question that Lithium Technologies answers for their clients. Katy Keim is CMO at Lithium, where their technology enables client "superfans" to drive the conversation. Their customer set includes Verizon, Google, Sephora, BestBuy and dozens of other international companies.

"These brands all believed that 'Company Brand' = X, and it was all about consistency, frequency and differentiation," Katy explains, as we talked about some of the common misconceptions in the field of marketing.

"There are a number of challenges in today's world, because channels are so fragmented," Katy says, unapologetically.

So frequency has changed, and branding has become all about reputation. Lithium enables reputation – they help empower others to say things about you. Online, and in forums where everyone looks for information – whether you watch TV on your laptop or Netflix gives you your entertainment feed, there's one place everyone turns for information and insights:

The customer comments section.

Lithium creates an online review mechanism that goes beyond the comments found on Yelp and the traditional customer reviews (although their cloud-based solutions do enable the kinds of comments and interactivity that you would expect on a site such as BestBuy.com, for example).

But Lithium enables "super fans" to become brand advocates – and, in many cases, take over much of the customer service functions required online.

"The brand is actually a better reflection of truth, in this day and age – truth about the products, truth about the services, truth about what the company actually stands for," Katy says.

In order to control that conversation online, companies have to make sure that their products, services and interactions are consistent. While the customer conversations can't be controlled, they can be influenced – influenced with quality across every aspect of the organization.

As Katy explains, "Online comments may not be the exact words that a marketing executive would choose, but the comments are an accurate reflection of the brand." Within a context of customer-created content, there is a greater trust in the marketplace, and a greater reflection of the true essence of a brand.

And certain customers have a very loud and honest voice. Take Lenovo, for example – an important Lithium reference customer.

At Lenovo, a team of customer volunteers staffs their customer service support site.

That's right: 100% of their customer support is provided by a worldwide team of volunteers. These individuals have built the company's "knowledge base" of online articles, and more.

According to Lithium's online documents, "we have focused on the management of superfans, because all our experience and data has shown us that if you take care of the most important users, the rest will follow."

It's a more sophisticated take on the 80/20 rule, or the "long tail" of customer engagement. Accomplished through a complex gamification algorithm (assigning points for reputation, within the community as a whole as well as within specific areas of expertise) desired input is rewarded and encouraged.

Superfans are identified. Super support is provided.

How are you rewarding your customers for their feedback?

How does that reward system help your organization to facilitate exchange?

Empowerment and enablement, Lithium style. The Lithium SaaS (Software as a Service) platform empowers a photography expert to review high-powered telephoto lenses, for example, and provide guidance and advice on a customer site – it's a personalized perspective, from an expert, that empowers a consumer to make an informed decision.

And Katy notes that there is a "halo" of individuals who see/observe the conversation – although they are not necessarily in the market for telephoto lenses, they are observing wise counsel and authentic advice from a particular online expert (or several online experts). The information in the forums may not lead these "halo" customers to an immediate buying decision, but the clarity of the conversation creates trust in a way that company-created content cannot. So the one-to-one conversation (between the expert and the curious telephoto lens shopper) has a ripple effect that can be easily measured in terms of trust and exchange online.

How is it measured? Page views. Comments. Interaction.

According to Lithium's surveys, customer feedback/new ideas were listed as the original purpose of visiting a community 46% of the time. However, new ideas and feedback were listed as a realized benefit 78% of the time.

Statistically, that's what a halo looks like.

"If you're Canon, for example, and you're looking at the thousands of interactions online - and you're a marketing person, looking at the vast amount of information, you've got to be thinking, 'Do you know how much of our community conversation focuses on lenses?' We should be producing content on lenses, we should be doing promotions on lenses, we should be talking at our trade shows about lenses. The traditional focus group is too slow and too limiting." But the online community is real-time, and real important, if you want to know what your brand is really doing.

Working with Lithium, Verizon launched a new product by reaching out to 100 customers and asking them, "How are we going to market this?"

If you are a marketer (and by the way, if you have a job, or you are looking for a job, or require oxygen to keep yourself alive, you are in marketing) consider what Lithium learned from working with Verizon.

What's the difference between telling the customer how they should feel about your brand, pushing things out to the market, and asking the customer: How can I engender an experience that translates how I want you to feel about me?

In other words, how can you create an experience for your customer that creates exchange? And then: how do you measure that experience? Because, let's face it, it's hard to measure how you feel about me. But, as my friend Jeffrey Hayzlett says, "Nothing says 'I love you' like a wire transfer."

Exchange is created where marketing makes money, but engendering a positive conversation is the first step – the *first* exchange. Feelings lead to revenues, which leads to repeat business, loyalty and other aspects of a bulletproof brand.

In fact, the heart drives the head in our decision process.

If you are analytical in nature, you may find that statement a little preposterous. You may not believe that the heart is in charge, and that our emotions (not our intellect) drive our decisions. But this counter-intuitive description still fits for even the most analytical among us.

I am suggesting that the soul drives the spreadsheet. If you don't believe me, just try buying a house with my wife.

Do you think I present her with a spreadsheet, demographic data, and an outline of which properties will make the most sense for our 2.4 children?

(We actually only have two children, but I think of them as exceptional, so – in my mind - that math actually works out. In fact my numbers may be a little low).

The spreadsheet only comes into play AFTER she says, "Oh my God! I LOVE IT!" or some similar version of that last statement. THEN the analysis and the hard work really begins.

Of course there is the matter of the budget.

Of course there is the matter of the bank financing.

Of course there is the matter of the neighborhood, the services and the schools.

But, first things first: you have to wait for the "OMG!" moment. Because it's good to have God on your side – especially when your significant other lets you know that you are on the right emotional track. Without that track, well, being a data jockey doesn't really matter.

Trust me on this. Or, better yet, trust yourself.

For marketers, branding is about statistics and numbers. Effective marketing is measurable, if you have the right data points.

But bulletproof branding begins with the conversation. Enabling that exchange allows you to have the right data points!

Build that on-demand, real-time conversation, if you want to create greater engagement. Build a brand around brand advocates – it's the only authentic answer, if you want to be bulletproof.

Patricia Seybold, in her book *Outside Innovation,* asks if you can harness customer innovation for competitive advantage – and the answer may surprise you. "You no longer win by having the smartest engineers and scientists; you win by having the smartest customers."

Seybold explains that customers have jobs they need to get done – not products they need to buy. Think about it for a second: what happens just before you go shopping, either online or in person? You've got a job to do.

Maybe that job is to make sure your kids have the right clothes for school.

Maybe that job is to make sure you have the right shoes for the big party on Saturday night.

Or maybe that job is to make sure you've got the right enterprise software solution for your multi-national organization, including a customized ship to bill module, by next year.

Customers think in terms of outcomes – problems that need solutions. A customer doesn't think in terms of products or services. So why should your organization?

When it comes time to hire an employee, all organizations everywhere look for the same thing: solutions providers. Doesn't matter if it's Raytheon (looking for someone who can help deliver the next big satellite) or Denny's (looking for someone who can help deliver the next big breakfast).

Companies need solutions providers.

And so do consumers.

As you consider the branding conversation, consider the solution that you provide. Are you able to articulate your brand value in terms of a solution?

Here are the key components, explained as an exercise that can help you to determine your true solution.

Step 1: Explain what your company does in the most literal fashion. Examples: "Our company provides financial services to institutional investors." "We install audio video equipment in hospitals and urgent care facilities in the Pacific Northwest." "Our company has been in business since 1923, providing land surveys in Southwest Louisiana." Got it in just one sentence? OK, let's shift the focus to what your customer is thinking.

Step 2: Ask yourself the same question your customer wants to know. Namely: if I have _____(fill in the blank with the product or service you offer), what do I really have, in terms of a solution? In other words, with your "23 years of experience" or "audio video equipment" or whatever else in the picture: what can I do? What do I really have?

Step 3: Now, take that question to a deeper level, from the perspective of the customer: What can I do differently? What can I do better – either more effectively, more efficiently, or more inexpensively?

Step 4: Why would your customer want to do that - that thing or things you just identified in Step 3? In other words:

What's the difference between "providing land surveys" and "making sure your commercial construction project starts off on the right foot?"

The phrasing is important. It's more than just semantics, more than just words. While both descriptions are factual, the latter choice represents a phrasing that considers what your customer is seeking.

Turn the mirror around when you think about your business. See things from the customer's perspective. See their needs first, if you want to truly understand your value proposition.

Explaining what you do is not as compelling as what you can do for others. Particularly when "others" are part of a group persona I like to call your Chief Branding Officer.

- Being descriptive is not the same as creating exchange.
- Providing information is not the same as providing solutions.
- Sending out a message is not the same as starting a conversation.

As you think about your experience, and your expertise, consider how well you really know your customer. Business skills, experience and intelligence are important to your career, and mine – but what matters most to the customer are the outcomes that you can create.

Think about the conversation you want to create:

What you do vs. *what problem can you solve*?

WHEN BRANDING GETS PERSONAL

A big portion of my work around branding focuses on a more personal subject: namely, personal branding. As the national elevator pitch champion, I'm often called upon to help create messages that can impact a career – providing the language of leadership, so that key employees can maximize their contribution. So, if your compensation matters to you, you've got to be interested in better personal branding. Today, everyone is a brand, and – since you are now the President and CEO of a brand called YOU - you have to have a message that cuts through the noise. You've got to be able to create a conversation around you – but it can't be self-serving!

Does that sound counter-intuitive?

The point is: your personal brand is not about what you can do. It's about what you can do for others. Your value proposition must be phrased in terms of the customers, clients and companies you wish to serve.

That value comes from effectively sharing your own thought leadership – the guidance, advice and insights that go beyond just a repetitive broadcast message.

I was working with a college audience and asked a young gent to stand up and deliver his elevator pitch. "Tell me a little bit about yourself," I said, offering the perfect softball for a personal branding statement.

Without hesitation he said, "I'm nine shades of awesome. Which color do you want first?"

Do you ever feel like opening a six-pack of unearned confidence is the best way to start the conversation? The only thing that's clear is that you need a little bit of self-awareness.

If someone is curious to know more about who you are, the first stop is online. In just the same way that people learn more about the products and services they care about, you will be Googled! In a business context, that means that you will undoubtedly be found on LinkedIn. For anyone in business today, LinkedIn is a vital platform for defining and establishing your personal brand.

Here are three sites that can help you to go beyond LinkedIn, in terms of creating a powerful personal profile. If you want to generate more awareness (and better search engine results) for yourself, consider these sites, in no particular order:

- **About.me** – about.me makes it easy for people to learn about you and access your content. For creative types, techies and craftsman entrepreneurs, there's no reason not to have an about.me page. Setup is about as easy as it can be, with an intuitive online tool. My page is right here: http://about.me/chriswestfall.

- **Twylah.com** – get a free Twitter assessment, and make sure your tweets get indexed and identified the right way, with Twylah. This Twitter tool is more than just content curation for your online profile – with advanced brand assessment tools, Twylah helps you to identify your message and control your brand more effectively. My profile is http://www.twylah.com/westfallonline.

BrandYourself.com – have you ever wondered what you could do to influence what people find when they Google you? BrandYourself.com is an easy-to-use profile management tool – especially useful if you have some negative publicity out there on the web. BrandYourself can help you to emphasize the positive, and influence search engine results, with a number of advanced tools. The free offering is feature-rich, and the pay-to-play model has some really terrific tools for you to consider. My profile is http://chriswestfall.brandyourself.com.

Chapter 3: Clarity

Judge a man by his questions, rather than his answers.

VOLTAIRE

We thought we had the answers, but it was the questions we had wrong.

BONO

HOW DO YOU KNOW if your message is clear? When it comes to your branding, it's easy to fall into a delusional trap around your messaging. You may think your story is clear, but until you receive confirmation, your story isn't bulletproof. Think about the conversations you have, on a daily basis that let you know exactly where you stand. For the people that matter most to you (your boss, your partner, your employees), that kind of clarity is what we all want – and it comes from a two-way communication.

Ultimately, clarity is your responsibility. And being clear about your own message is a requirement for the digital age. Your career, your compensation and your contribution all begin with your ability to be clear.

That's the premise of Marcus Buckingham's book, *The One Thing You Need to Know*. (I don't want to spoil it for you, but …there's actually more than one thing you need to know).

Buckingham's premise is clear: the one common element that all leaders possess is clarity. Don't think of yourself as a leader? Well, that's understandable – but if you wish to influence and persuade others, you are seeking the two key components of leadership.

And the one thing you've got to have, if you want to be heard above the likes, tweets and pokes, is a clear message.

Clarity requires confirmation.

Confirmation can only come from one place.

Confirmation comes from the customer.

If you want to know if your message is clear, stop broadcasting.

Start listening.

Let's take a look at the back half of the conversation – the part of the story that's often forgotten in the marketing mix.

Are you ready to listen?

One of the most iconic brands in the world is Cisco - a provider of products and services, most notably many of the devices that form the backbone of the internet, the infrastructure for corporate networks, and a wide range of solutions for video conferencing.

Cisco CEO John Chambers has often cited the importance of listening to the customer as the key to Cisco's success as a brand. "If you listen to the customer," Chambers says, "they will tell you everything you need to be successful."

That's according to Karen Mangia, the Senior Director of the Listening Services Center of Excellence (LSCOE) at Cisco. In her role, she oversees the importance of active listening across the partner and customer channels, as well as internally.

According to Karen, listening to customers (and then doing something with that feedback) is how Cisco finds "true north" – that direction and focus for current events, and future strategies.

And that true north can't come from the inside out – in other words, it's not about what Cisco wants customers to say about the company.

The real story is what customers, partners and employees say about the company.

So, where did the idea for the Listening Center come from?

"About three years ago," Mangia explains, "we started hearing in a variety of surveys and feedback tools – ranging from actual customers coming into our executive briefing centers, comments on surveys, and other methods –we started hearing this idea that it was becoming difficult to do business with Cisco.

"We weren't necessarily asking specific questions about 'ease of doing business,' but it started emerging as a theme.

"The really important thing to do was to find out more: what was driving the perception [that doing business with Cisco was difficult]?

"So we started asking some questions through a variety of listening vehicles about that [difficulty]."

Customer satisfaction is a top priority at the company. In fact, customer satisfaction is a driving force behind the company's bonus and incentive structure – for every employee worldwide.

And the surveys – both internal and external - were telling a similar story. Doing business with Cisco was becoming more and more difficult - whether as a customer, partner or employee.

Poor survey results begged the question: what drives that perception of the ease of doing business with Cisco?

Think about the Cisco customer for a second. That customer is trying to get their equipment on time - the right equipment at the right time, exactly as promised and expected.

When a customer has a support issue, no matter what piece of gear or software, that individual has expectations. And, for a Fortune 100 company like Cisco, those expectations can be high.

The customer wants to know that if there's a service issue or question about the equipment, the person who picks up the phone knows exactly what is installed at the customer's premise.

The customer wants to know that the service representative knows the exact terms and coverage for the service contract, for example.

 Think about that for a company that has multiple locations, multiple data centers, and multiple video conferencing facilities. Managing complexity is now woven into your branding. Because managing and meeting expectations is key to making your brand bulletproof.

Expediting the service process hinges on insight and expertise that acknowledges the customers' situation – and that level of detail and awareness is as much a technological challenge as it is a personal one.

Not many businesses have the layers of complexity found within Cisco. But perhaps you are wondering if your organization has the kind of insights needed to meet your customers' expectations. And, if you're not wondering about customer expectations, you should be.

Are you really listening? Because your customer has the message you need to hear!

Listen to what changed at Cisco, as they began listening not only to customers, but to their partners – the resellers responsible for selling, installing and servicing a large portion of Cisco's business:

"What we discovered," Karen explains, "was that we had this very homogenous viewpoint of what 'ease of doing business' meant.

"We sort of thought 'ease' meant the same thing for everyone."

Have you ever experienced a moment of unexpected clarity, when you listen to your customers? At Cisco, allowing customers to participate in the definition of one of their core principles created a significant change in their business processes.

"One size fits all" was replaced with a new framework for defining processes throughout the organization. Here's how it happened:

1. **Cisco Started Paying Attention:** The organization made a conscious and deliberate effort to watch customer and partner satisfaction scores for a year. The emphasis? Making it easier to do business with Cisco.

2. **The CEO Started Paying MORE than Attention:** Sponsored by Chambers, a formalized process for tracking was put into place. And, to make sure

everyone was on the same page, Chambers tied the results to everyone's compensation. New targets were introduced, based on objective statistical criteria. Those numbers universally changed the numbers on every employee's W-2.

3. **Accounting for Accountability:** Senior executive leaders were assigned responsibility for monitoring and impacting the drivers. The company developed a "Top 10 List" of initiatives around the most common and acute problems. And company Vice Presidents were assigned responsibility for change. Every quarter, the executive in charge of a particular area would be asked to "stand and deliver" a report to senior leadership.

4. **Driving the Drivers:** Using a statistical regression analysis model (a fancy way of using math to identify if statistics are more than just coincidences, and to identify common threads among different sets of data), leadership identified areas for consolidation, elimination and improvement – all focused on simplifying the process, and making it easier to do business with Cisco. Most importantly, the organization looked at the findings and changes that wouldn't correlate – in other words, rejecting activities that would not influence what the customer was saying.

Because Cisco sells equipment, as well as other solutions, sometimes customers want to try out a particular piece of gear at their location before they actually buy.

Do you know any customer who would rather try before they buy? Putting product in the customer's hands is the classic sales strategy. There are different ways to describe the "try before you buy" strategy – but I call it the "Puppy Strategy."

If you want to sell somebody a puppy, put that cute animal in their hands.

And if you're really serious about a transaction, give the puppy to their kids.

The result of this attention and accountability produced some compelling results. Namely, a consistent difficulty emerged around the demonstration equipment program. Basically, Cisco has a program where customers can check out equipment – think of it as a lending library for electronic equipment – to try out the performance, installation and other criteria within a customer's existing infrastructure.

Consistent feedback indicated that customers were taking too much time to return equipment, and that meant that others couldn't check it out.

And if customers couldn't try, they couldn't buy.

Karen's team gathered data and feedback, and received no less than 38 recommendations from the customer channel – ways to streamline the process.

Cisco took all 38 recommendations and put them into place.

The result? The amount of cycle time was significantly reduced, and equipment was returned to "the library" more quickly.

That acceleration translated into a 13% year-over-year increase in demonstrations, because the equipment was more available for utilization.

But here's the real key to the success of the program, and an important insight into what listening really means:

"The way we really reduced cycle times," Karen explains, "happened after the surveys and the questions. We took the information provided in the interview process and we said to our customers, 'We took the information you gave us, with the 38 areas of improvement. We implemented all 38 suggestions, and here are the results we are seeing because of your feedback.'"

Closing the loop is key, if you're really listening.

Providing feedback and demonstrating action is the real key to the conversation. Especially if you are changing a process that's been in place for a long time.

Actions are the best response to expectations, wouldn't you agree?

For customers at Cisco, the feeling was, "Oh, you listened to me, and you actually used my feedback, and you're right: there is a better result."

What would those sentiments mean for your brand? How could listening – and "closing the loop" – create a bulletproof brand for your organization?

Coincidentally, if you don't turn ideas into action, people will stop giving you their ideas.

> *Sell your knowledge, and*
> *purchase bewilderment.*
>
> RUNI

Questions without consequence will make your customers resent your surveys and your requests. "Why are you asking me these questions, when I know you won't do anything with the information I provide to you?"

So, even though your organization may not have the resources of a multi-national like Cisco, what can you do – right now – to make sure you're really listening?

Here are three things you can do, today, to make sure your branding is bulletproof:

1. **Go Formal:** Create a formalized program on how you are going to make your customers successful. The cycle of your success begins with your customer. Put a process in place, with visibility and accountability. And make sure that the program has the endorsement, support and expectation of the CEO. Otherwise, branding is an initiative within your organization – instead of an initiative throughout the organization. How will your program impact every person within your company? It's no secret that what gets measured gets done. And tying success to a paycheck is a clear message, if the customer's satisfaction is the key to making your brand bulletproof.

2. **Question Everything:** Even if you're only going to ask your customers one question, and that question is: "How likely are you to recommend our products and services to someone else?" you have to credibly demonstrate that you have done (or will do) something with the feedback that they give to you. Otherwise, they are not going to trust you with more. What plans or processes will you use to "close the loop" - to let your customers know what changed because of their feedback?

3. **Don't Let the Inmates Run the Asylum:** If you receive feedback that is unrealistic, or contrary to your business plans, say so. Feedback deserves an honest response. If a request or suggestion is not possible within your current portfolio of solutions,

say so. False hopes are just that: false. Let your customers know where you stand, and that you're listening. Of course, listening is not the same as granting wishes. Be honest and straightforward in your feedback, and start working – today – to make sure you close the loop on your listening.

Active listening means putting stories into action. How do you listen to your customers? More importantly, how do you use customer information to create new results? .

TIGHTEN THE STORY

Before I refuse to take your questions, I have an opening statement.

RONALD REGAN

One of the greatest lessons I learned came from a discovery I made in graduate school. At TCU (that's Texas Christian University), the focus of the MBA program was on group work: when it was time to take your final, you shared your grade with three other team members. And group presentations (both oral and written) were always on the agenda, whether you liked it or not.

And everyone in your group got the same grade.

The experience mirrored the world of business: a single superstar or lone ranger can't create bulletproof branding. The story has to be a unified effort. Your story is told by a group, and that group is either cohesive… or your result will be a complete failure.

It was finals time, first semester. Our assignment was to create a new product for an existing business, and deliver a corresponding marketing plan with all the segmentation and other accoutrements.

Instead of focusing solely on everyone's role within the presentation, like actors rehearsing our parts, we decided to focus instead on the unknown. We concentrated on the questions that we would receive.

- We considered what questions we knew we would hear.
- Then we focused on the questions we would love to hear.
- And then, what questions we would learn to fear!

Do you know what questions you would love to hear from your customers? Beyond the usual suspects of "How much does it cost?" and "Where can I buy it?," what are the questions you are currently answering for your clientele?

Are you answering a question that no one has asked?

Are you sending out a message that makes people say, "So what?" instead of "Send me some!"

The Socratic method uses questions to create discourse. There's great wisdom in the questions that come up within the conversation. Find your favorites – and your fears – and take time to get clear on your responses.

Chapter 4: Collaboration

Talent wins games, but teamwork and intelligence wins championships.

MICHAEL JORDAN

I think it is in collaboration that the nature of art is revealed.

AMERICAN MUSICIAN STEVE LACY

HOW CAN AN ORGANIZATION with over 140,000 employees create a bulletproof brand?

And what could be learned from the branding strategies that drive over $2 billion in net income, worldwide?

That's what I wondered when I spoke with Mike Fernandez, Vice President for Corporate Affairs at Cargill.

In case you are unfamiliar: Cargill is the largest privately held corporation in the United States. And it's a family-owned, family-run business.

With revenues over $136 billion in 2013, Cargill would be number 9 on the Fortune 500, if it were a public company. And, with diverse interests all over the world, the organization has layers of complexity that present a particular problem. Namely, how do you unify and connect a brand message for such a large organization?

Enter Mike Fernandez.

Mike's responsibilities include government relations, media, communications, marketing services and yes, you guessed it: brand management. He started with Cargill in 2010 after a career that took him to State Farm Insurance, ConAgra Foods, CIGNA, and US WEST (now known as CenturyLink). With a diverse background in public affairs, PR and marketing, he brings a unique perspective to this international giant – a company that, in all fairness, has received its share of criticism over the years.

So, I wondered: How does Cargill use collaboration in its marketing?

What can we learn from this massive global organization? And how has Cargill created its own version of bulletproof branding?

Here's what Mike had to say when I asked him about the difference between branding and reputation at Cargill:

> **Mike Fernandez:** My orientation around communications, marketing, branding really evolved from an early career in politics, then the Eastman Kodak Company. In an earlier day, I would have said that the difference between brand and reputation was pretty clear for me. You would say a brand is really related to products and services - it was related to the company's promise. Reputation was what the public believed. So the brand was what you wanted to be, and reputation is how the public perceived it to be.
>
> As one conceives of one's own brand positioning and what you want it to be, you really have to go through a pretty in-depth exercise in making sure it's authentic and true to who you are and that your employees and closest stakeholders believe it. And to the extent that the brand is aspirational, you better have some "bread crumbs" so people have some visibility that you're headed in a particular direction. Otherwise you're going to be more quickly discovered and found out as a fraud.

Before, brands used to be about logos and slogans for a lot of people. And now it's more about behavior. Branding is not only about what you do but how you do it.

So, in that mix, it prompts you to think about whether you need to move the bar up in terms of what you currently think of as transparency.

In other words: in terms of what you share about what you do, who you are, and what your intentions are.

I would argue that in decades past, the exercise of developing a brand was almost a one-way exercise.

While I agree, I had to point out that this kind of silo exercise can't work within an organization like Cargill – because of the nature of the food processing business. Relying on partners and serving stakeholders simultaneously can be a lot to handle – particularly from a branding perspective. Here's how Mike responds:

MF: We listen to a lot of various stakeholders, not the least of which is our owners, since we are a privately held company. And for us, that's also interesting just in terms of the growth of the family's thoughts. A certain number of family members, their last name is on the company. For those whose last name is not, they are descendants of someone who was. So they are very sensitive to making sure we operate in the best way.

Cargill is a company where people are very concerned about ethics. From day one, every employee gets something called our guiding principles. It has a quote in there from the second leader of the company that essentially says "our word is our bond," then it marches through seven principles. The seventh one is the most important to our topic but all of them are important:

1. We obey the law
2. We conduct our business with integrity
3. We keep accurate and honest records
4. We honor our business obligations
5. We treat people with dignity and respect
6. We protect Cargill's information, assets and interest …but the last one is:
7. We are committed to being a responsible global citizen.

So, inherently, on Day One, the thought pattern is to get employees thinking about their responsibilities relative to the brand and reputation of the enterprise.

Is Cargill able to fulfill on these promises?

After all, part of collaboration is giving back – and making sure that you manage your partnerships and your supply chain in a way that makes sense for everyone involved.

MF: And admittedly, I would say [the concept of global impact] has only grown over time, if we are being honest and transparent. Yes, in some ways the ethic of corporate social responsibility is part of the Cargill culture, probably long before those "social responsibility" words were actually used. Our founder, William Wallace Cargill, back in 1865[1], talked about integrity. He talked about responsible business practices. We can find records going back to the early 1900s, like 1911, where the company is giving relief money to Europe. After World War I the [Cargill family] created a foundation and put some structure around a relief effort. And then when you had the famine in India in 1965 that prompted the United States government to develop the Food for Peace program in 1966, Cargill - being in part a grain trading business - got even more active with corporate philanthropy.

Then, in the 1980s, we actually built more structure around conscientious giving, so that there was a real thought pattern to corporate contributions worldwide. Today, we're constantly sitting down with various NGOs[2] and public policy makers and discerning what can we do to move the edge on sustainability of products.

We need to do things that are environmentally smart and socially smart. Because we want our business to be sustainable for future generations of stakeholders.

So, branding has to be a collaborative exchange.

In other words, what you say about yourself is only as good as what you deliver. Certainly the social responsibility, the involvement in the community helps to create that bulletproof brand – and builds on the concept of collaboration. But, is there a way that marketers can influence other areas of the organization? For example, if you're doing a great job of branding and sharing the conversation, but the execution's not there, then what?

Bulletproof branding isn't just a part of your business – it *is* your business.

Marketing has to have a broader reach, both internally and externally, to fulfill on the value of the organization. That means even greater collaboration – greater buy-in – than ever before.

So, I asked Mike: Are there ways that marketing and branding can have a broader reach? How do you achieve that greater connection?

> **MF:** I would say that businesses actually invite us into the discussion in a way that you wouldn't have seen years ago. Our corporate responsibility team is often overseeing both the public relations side of the house and the marketing side of the house.

How does that linkage manifest itself in the marketplace and in your branding?

> **MF:** I'm increasingly called upon to bring in my corporate social responsibility team by Cargill business units, and there are 72 of them, to make

presentations on our point of view on things like sustainability, food security, responsible supply chains, to their customers! So [the conversation has] come full circle. Now we're partnering in discussions with a Walmart or a McDonald's or with a Unilever or with a Nestle because we see [this global collaboration] as a world in which we're part of their supply chain. Just as we're wanting to advance our brand, we only really do well advancing our brand if we're also cognizant [of collaboration] - that what we're dealing with, if we act badly, will have downstream negative impacts on all of their brands.

So, it's all interconnected. And then, at the same time, we're oftentimes brokering discussions between NGOs and public policy makers. We engage our engineers, who are building new facilities or reconfiguring facilities to consider the implications. As a result, we're now in the business where we're capturing biogas, and we're operating the [food processing] plants more efficiently with less energy, with fewer inputs. We're recycling water that's used in the process of making food. In many instances, we're returning energy to the grid. It is very holistic.

Thirty years ago, the idea of corporate responsibility was, well, "We write checks to causes that we think are interesting and that some of our people care about."

Fast forward to now, where it's not about just writing checks. Those checks are written with a more focused agenda.

And what is that agenda?

MF: We talk about fewer, bigger, better.

We're going to do fewer things in a bigger way in order to make a better difference for the partners we're engaged with and ultimately for our customers. That impact reaches public policy makers and the NGOs of the world.

And that perspective is interspersed with how we think about the brand of the company.

For a company like ours where we're essentially a B2B - we do have retail products like Truvia - but as a B2B, we're saying (almost like John McMillan Sr. said many years ago), our word is our bond.[3]

What is enveloped in our brand promise is trust. Our largest customers trust us to deliver for them anywhere in the world. They trust us in a way that they believe in doing business with us. Literally, by interacting with Cargill, they believe they will be better off.

How are you communicating that message of trust, without sounding too "grand" in terms of the value Cargill provides?

MF: We want to do our best to deliver to the various stakeholders that we have, and then the brand message is that we want them to be confident that when they work with us, whether it's a product or service, that they're going to be the beneficiaries, that they're going to thrive.

We're kind of at an interesting point where actually that's going to be the word going forward for us - and that word is "thrive." And in derivations of that [message] in multiple languages across the world.

And what does "thrive" mean in the Cargill context, exactly?

MF: "Thrive" gives you the sense you've got a word that's about having not just one good deal. Thrive is about *now*. And health and vitality going forward. The notion of "thrive" is: we want to be there to help various parties flourish in a way that's beneficial to them, and beneficial to the world.

So, it's not a tagline, it's incorporated into how we think. When we talk about how we organize ourselves internally, we went through an exercise where we developed kind of a strategic intent statement. The end result was what we say about ourselves:

Cargill will be the partner of choice recognized as having great people with imagination, committed to delivering the best ideas to the worlds we serve: agriculture, food and risk management.

So, as we think about our brand, it really is enveloped in that phrase "partner of choice."

But branding is more than just a slogan, and more than what you say about yourself. Can you give any examples of how you took this idea from the page to the stage? In other words, where there is actual evidence in the marketplace that goes beyond just a mission statement?

MF: I think that there are two interesting examples that have been shaping up that get into how the brand is becoming an element of how we manage and how we do things. In Brazil, we have a thriving soy business but there were lots of concerns around farming in Mato Grosso.[4] The concerns focused on those areas around and near the Amazon as to whether they were having any negative impact on the Amazon. So, we're working with all of these farmers and, at the same time, this is going back before my time, they had some challenges from Greenpeace and other NGOs that were concerned. And rather than getting involved in a long, drawn-out, bitter battle, they started talking to Greenpeace and they started talking to other NGOs and ultimately what they did is they got agreement on what the standards for sustainability should be and worked with the government to get them codified and worked with NGOs. And then they actually invited an NGO in to monitor the farms they were dealing with directly such that today we have satellite imagery of all of those farms. And if a farmer cuts down a tree they're not supposed to or burns something down they're not supposed to, or they treat the farm workers poorly, they're out of our program. We won't buy soy from them. And in that part of the world, we're basically their primary ticket to sell that soy. So, here you actually have an NGO, the Nature Conservancy, working with us and we're working with them, to both preserve the Amazon while at the same time preserving sustainable farming of soy.

So, essentially, Cargill is helping the farmers to be better by keeping an eye on things?

MF: Yeah, but also they know what we're looking at, so it's a partnership. It's not so much that we're sitting there with a billy club. They get it, they understand. When I first joined the company and went down to Brazil and met with some of the farmers, they told the tale about when all these NGOs were beginning to gum up the works and make it difficult for soy to move out of the region, all of a sudden Cargill had an NGO show up on their doorstep to try and help them. At first they thought Cargill was crazy. And, once they worked through it, they found out they could get the kinds of yields that they needed. They found out that they could be successful while also being sustainable. Further, we've made a commitment that the palm oil that we provide to much of the Western world, by 2015 will all be sustainable, RSPO certified, and that by 2020, all of what we supply to the world will be sustainable, in terms of palm oil.

Back in the early 1980s, a guy by the name of James Grunig[5] configured something that was called the four models of public relations. He described the press agency publicity model and the public information model – these kinds of one-way, asymmetrical methods of communication. He started talking back then [in the 1980s] that he believed the most successful models of the future would be two-way symmetrical models, where you would have dialogue, you'd have negotiation, you'd work to resolve conflict and promote mutual understanding and respect between various types of organizations and publics.

Those early writings were predicting in part what we see through social media. But by and large, two-way communication is what we're seeing in this world in which behaviors and how we do things are more important to brand reputation than what we do.

So, because of Grunig, social media, and the environment you've described: how we do things is more important than what we do?

> **MF:** Maybe not more important, at least as important.

In that context, how would you answer this question: What percentage of business issues would you classify as communication issues?

> **MF:** (*laughing*) Well, in some sense, all of them! Certain constituencies are going to be more moved or concerned about certain types of issues than

others. That's never going to change. An environmental NGO is going to be concerned about environmental issues. A consumer or customer might be most fundamentally impacted by price, or a factor of supply and demand, or whatever other perceived value is inherent in that product or service for them.

But, what we're also seeing is that the conversation about products and services is no longer one way. Other parties are shaping that every day. In some ways, the world of business is becoming more like the world of politics.

How so?

MF: In politics, communications is paramount because ultimately you have to communicate in a way that you get a market share that's fifty percent, plus one. There are lots of businesses that exist with market shares that are much smaller than fifty percent plus one.

The other challenge with the marketing of the product or the candidate as a product, is that a candidate is a vessel for lots of different issues and perspectives. You may be more interested in what that candidate has to say about education; I may be more interested in what that candidate has to say about immigration.

But at the end of the day, the confluence of multiple perceptions ultimately leads to a victor and a loser. And the challenge for products - and for companies - is that people are coming to understand that companies are purveyors of more than one product or service.

People also coming to understand that oftentimes products, especially at the consumer level, aren't mere commodities. Products [and services] have certain intrinsic values and sometimes multiple ingredients. So, supply chains begin to matter in terms of "Where did that product come from? What are the actual constituent ingredients in that product?" And more and more of that information is being shared more broadly – via social or other platforms – in real-time.

Thus, the quote from our CEO, Greg Page, "In a world where nothing can be hidden, you better not have anything to hide." So, the idea of brand and reputation is more dynamic than ever before. And it's being shaped from many more corners of the world. .

TIGHTEN THE STORY

How far does your brand reach? Considering the model that Mike discussed for Cargill, think about ways that you can connect your brand to your supply chain.

Take a moment to list the stakeholders for your brand. Leave out the usual suspects (your owners, your board of directors, your employees and stockholders) and focus on the businesses that are a part of your business.

How can you connect your brand in a way that creates a more positive experience for the businesses you work with?

How do you define "social responsibility," and what causes matter most to you and your organization? So many times, when you look at what an individual or an organization does for the less fortunate, you see where the company's values truly align.

For your brand message to really resonate, you want to make sure you create connections to the causes that fit for your values. After all, your core values are central to your brand – and wise support of causes that matter will influence the strength of your message.

After all, your customers, prospects and employees want to know where your company stands in relation to supporting and cultivating positive relationships. That idea has long been a part of Cargill's strategy – as well as the company's value chain.

List three causes that matter to your company:

1. _____
2. _____
3. _____

Now ask the important question, for each of these items listed above: *Why?*

Why do you support these causes?

How does your support reflect your company's core values? How does your engagement with something greater than the P&L statement add meaning to your brand?

Does your organization have more than one bottom line?

For your suppliers, your stakeholders, and your surroundings – consider the contribution you make, to the people that make your business run smoothly.

A bulletproof brand is a one that looks beyond the borders of the organization. Providing for the good of others, in some meaningful way, is key to crafting a quiet but powerful statement within the branding conversation.

Chapter 5: Context

Insight and foresight are linked with leadership. It's insight that helps to capture opportunity.

ZHOU MING, EXECUTIVE VICE PRESIDENT AND
SECRETARY GENERAL, CHINA COUNCIL FOR
INTERNATIONAL INVESTMENT PROMOTION

Social media is essential in the new Age of Context. It is in our online conversations that we make it clear what we like, where we are and what we are looking for.

THE AGE OF CONTEXT BY ROBERT SCOBLE
AND SHEL ISRAEL

A FEW YEARS AGO, IBM Global Services published a report called *Capitalizing on Complexity*.

IBM asked over 1500 global executives – business leaders from Asia, Europe and North America – to define the number one quality of leaders.

What do you think these business executives said was number one?

- Was it financial acumen?
- Was it charisma?
- Was it empathy?
- Was it communication skills?

No. None of the above.

The number one skill of leaders – according to IBM's survey – was *creativity*.

Not creativity in terms of "arts and crafts," or some sort of traditional creative pursuit.

But creativity: the process of creation.

Here's what IBM discovered:

> *The most successful organizations co-create products and services with customers, and integrate customers into core processes.*
>
> They are adopting new channels to engage and stay in tune with customers. By drawing more insight from the available data, successful CEOs make customer intimacy their number-one priority.

Effective leaders embody creative leadership – in other words, inviting disruptive innovation, encouraging others to drop outdated approaches and take calculated risks. And a top priority for these global CEOs: reinventing customer relationships.

IBM identified that co-creation with customers is a key area for differentiation, in an era of ever-increasing information overload.

Connecting with the customer community is paramount - in the spirit of creation.

That's the context for a new kind of creativity – and a new kind of business leadership.

Managing the brand conversation requires a context, just as all conversations need context in order to make sense.

The context happens within a community – also called an audience or a "public" that's interested in participation.

In other words, the folks that are creating the most important kind of exchange: the exchange of ideas, thoughts and communication around your brand.

Tim McDonald is the community manager for one of the most iconic brands in the world. The Huffington Post was ranked at the top of the Most Popular Political Sites, a ranking based on its Alexa Global Traffic Rank.[1]

With over one million comments on the site each month, the blog that Arianna Huffington started in 2005 has become a worldwide sensation and news resource. Within the organization, HuffPost Live is a live-streaming network, producing social video content around the clock. The organization produces 12 hours of original content, five days a week – shown live from 10am – 10pm ET (as of this writing).

In the spirit of social, the content is designed around the comments – a model that encourages participation and connection. HuffPost Live puts online viewers in contact with the guests on the show, in real-time – creating a one-of-a-kind live interactive experience.

Creating engagement within the community is the responsibility of Tim McDonald[2]. A Chicago native, Tim was lured to New York to create and develop a context for brand engagement – a context that focuses on multiple audiences within the Huffington Post universe.

I first connected with Tim via our mutual interest in a rapidly expanding blog, 12most.com. As the business editor, I had the opportunity to pull together from various authors and bloggers, and I always appreciated Tim's content. More importantly, I appreciated the way he stayed connected – really showing a savvy understanding of how social media can guide and encourage the conversation.

Evidently, Huffington Post noticed his impact as well. In fact, it was his online presence that attracted the brand to Tim, and they sought him out for this newly created position. His story is a classic tale of how a personal brand – if managed correctly – can turn into a career opportunity.

As community manager, Tim has a position that is still fairly rare, although gaining in popularity at some forward-thinking institutions. His job, really, is to facilitate the conversation around the brand.

Facilitating that conversation means:

- Creating engagement through relevant content
- Building online communities that focus on diverse interests
- Participating and encouraging the brand conversation

But there's more to community management than just creating a dialogue. That's why I had to have a dialogue with Tim, so I could share his viewpoint in his own words.

How does his perspective reflect your vision for your organization? How are you managing your community, and why does community management matter? Here's Tim's approach to branding, community management and more:

> **Tim McDonald:** So, I was at this conference, and before we started, they said, "What are you hoping to get out of it? What was most valuable to you?" etc. and that's when I had this realization. What if we stopped thinking of work as work, and start thinking of work as art?
>
> Think about it. What if we start creating things instead of producing things. I mean, they both have the same result, right? They both have a tangible product or service at the end. But what's happening now is when you create something, that thing has your passion inside of it. It has innovation inside of it. Because you weren't told "You have to fill out this form." You actually created something.
>
> You *created* this report, instead of just filling out a form. Those are the things that are going to start changing the workplace. We already have entrepreneurs, we have a workforce. But what we are going to start seeing is a lot more intrapreneurs.
>
> We're going to start seeing a more collaborative economy, a more shared economy. And enterprise businesses are going to take part in this, as we see their production facilities reduce, as workers have less to do, they [the enterprise] have traditional resources that they are not fully utilizing. Where

can they take advantage of that [reduction in utilization]? By partnering with other organizations that can benefit from their services.

Chris Westfall: Business is a process. Like a franchise organization – they all have to operate the same way to create the same consistent product. So, I agree with you in terms of creativity, but does that mean that process goes out the window, and every task becomes a science experiment?

TM: Not at all. Here's a perfect example of how passion is unique to every single one of us. If you go to a Starbucks, and I don't care which one, but if you go to a Starbucks, they have the same drinks, right? The same type of environment. The only thing that can differentiate [one Starbucks from another] is the people they have working for them.

Now, how many Starbucks have you been to in your life?

CW: More than I care to admit.

TM: But can you remember a couple of baristas that – just in your experience – made a difference?

And you can probably count them on one hand. But what a difference they make, don't they?

The barista makes that experience unique from every other Starbucks.

I don't care if every Starbucks has Wi-Fi. I don't care if every Starbucks has a comfortable couch to sit in, and I don't care if every one has the same exact temperature brewed coffee that I order every single time.

I'm going to go to the one where I have the best experience.

And that's where you start creating something – creating that experience that the customer has.

CW: So the experience happens through people. But, how does that translate online? How does that personal experience translate electronically, into a context that drives community?

TM: The way that I use social media, and the way that I encourage others to use social media, is to remember that you are an extension of yourself online. And I don't care whatever brand is out there and whatever message they are trying to craft, people online see right through it [if your message is inauthentic]. If you're putting up a false personality and blasting out messages without engaging with people, you might get retweets because you've got a clever headline in there. But ultimately you're not forming a relationship with [broadcasting].

CW: Can you talk about personal branding – how your personal brand created your role with Huffington Post? Your social media presence is what got you here. And now, it's gotten you moved into new roles, as you see the value of speaking to groups and investing your time in conferences and events, the organization has started investing, too.

TM: I don't think there's any such thing as work/life balance. I think it's more of a work/life blend. As I go out and speak, I might be building my own personal brand, but I'm also building the Huff Post brand. Because every time people know me, they know me as being [a representative of] Huffington Post. So what I bring and share from the stage represents Huffington Post as well as me personally.

CW: So what's that gravitational pull in your personal brand, that you created, that attracted the attention of the Huffington Post?

TM: You say gravitational pull; I call it a "magnet." It's all about drawing people in and attracting people to us. That's what we want to do with our personal brand, that's what we want to do with our work brand.

[Attraction is] the difference between what we've traditionally done in marketing and branding – being a bulldozer and pushing the message out – to becoming a magnet, drawing people in and making the attraction stick.

CW: That's the community manager aspect of it? Drawing the audience to you and then not letting them go?

TM: Yes.

You don't need a community manager to manage your social media. You need a community manager that understands that social media is a communication tool. And so therefore, what they [the effective community managers] are doing is recognizing that social media is a communication tool. They understand that what you are doing in building an online community relates back to the business goals.

CW: And social is a component of that. But it's not the whole island, so to speak.

TM: Do you have a telephone policy? Do you have an email policy?

CW: I answer the phone when it rings…I don't know. Should I have a phone policy, or an email policy?

TM: Why do we have a social media policy?

CW: Interesting! So, does that go back to what you were saying before, that people believe they need a social media policy because they don't know what will be said about them, about their brand?

TM: Yeah, because it's unknown right now. It's the Wild West. Nobody knows the rules. Nobody knows what's going to happen. But that's what makes it exciting at the same time, because we have this opportunity to create what we want while we can, and formulate it in the direction that we want [social media] to go. And the direction isn't going to be just another broadcast platform. People are always going to gravitate to where they can adapt their pain points.

CW: Shifting gears back to your role as a community manager. How do you define the community? What does community mean to you?

TM: I think any community is going to have some diversity to it, to be sustaining and healthy. I have really changed my thinking on this over time. Communities can come in different sizes and in different compositions, but the biggest part around [community] is that you can't try and force too many people and lose the core element of what the community does – which is the common thread that attracted all of those people in the first place. In other words, the original magnet that drew everyone together.

If I look at the concept of community within Huffington Post, it's very broad because we have over 70 different verticals. So the people that are interested in politics aren't necessarily interested in sports. And the people in sports aren't necessarily interested in science. The people in science aren't necessarily interested in parenting issues. And so, we might have some crossovers in communities but each one is its own unique subset within the greater community and they might not want to have anything to do with one another. So really I think it's to identify what the community is there for, and then make sure you are delivering something of value to them to make them want to stay.

When I say "value," I don't mean you have to go create coupons, offer discounts or give freebies away. Often when you start incentivizing true advocates of your brand, you desensitize them because now they feel that they should be compensated for everything they do.

CW: So the knowledge exchange is its own reward?

TM: Right, it's an emotional thing. It's not transactional.

CW: You mentioned earlier about how you can turn a community into brand advocates with making it a "one-click-away" model. Can you explain that model?

TM: It's not that you can turn your whole community into brand advocates... but there are certain people within your community that you can actually turn into brand advocates. And the one concern, the one fear that organizations have is that they say, "Well, this is great but how can I have these people go out and spread my message for me when I can't tell them what to say?" But the whole thing that you can do is – if you want them to share stuff – use the KISS method. "Keep it simple, stupid."

They [the audience of brand advocates] don't need to think about what message they are going to share, they are just going to share by clicking the button. You already have a pre-populated tweet with the words that you want to go out, you're not making them stop to think, you're making it as simple as you can for them. They push [the button] and your message is going out. So it's all about just keeping it simple, and [if you do it right, your audience of potential brand advocates] views it as, "You're helping me out. You're making it easy for me now. You're giving me pictures to download. You're giving me content that I can just click and share on my social networks – you're not making me do any work for you."

CW: There's a trust factor in there, isn't there?

TM: Oh yeah – because if you ever break that trust, you'll never get it back. It's very difficult to repair.

CW: How can organizations be sure that they don't break that trust? What are some cautionary tales or mistakes that you've seen?

TM: One of the golden rules that I live by and a question I always ask myself is, "What is my community going to think of this?"

CW: But that's kind of a paradox, isn't it? Because you don't want to operate based on what other people think.

TM: You don't want to worry about what they think, but if you know your job and you know your community you know what they're thinking about.

CW: So it's more about staying focused, vs. being insecure about how they might react?

TM: Right. You can't be insecure about the way that they will react. And the biggest thing is that, way too often in our own business minds, we think, "What's in it for us? What do you [yourself] want to get out of it?" If we just switch that around and ask what do they [the community] want to get out of a particular piece of content or experience, and then deliver that, you don't break that trust. The trust starts to get broken when we start to think about what's in it for us instead of what's in it for our community.

CW: So true! You have to stay on message and focus on the value that you are creating for your audience. It's an instantaneous built-in A-B test, because an active community will tell you right away if you are on message, right?

TM: Absolutely. Reminds me of the time I was going to give this B2B talk and I was so worried – because, when I stop to think about it, I really have been in more B2C industries than I have B2B. I always speak with other people on topics that are almost always B2C. So this was the first time I was speaking to a B2B audience.

And the person before me spoke about ROI – you know, numbers. The person after me was speaking about all numbers as well. And here I come with no numbers, lots of pictures, lots of touchy feel stuff, lots of emotional stuff. But the funny thing about it was, they all got it. My presentation resonated with them. Because they started understanding that when you talk about finding advocates, this isn't about finding one million advocates. It's about finding the 10 or the 50 or 100 advocates that are really going to turn your message up for you. What would you rather do – have one million people reached through 50 people who are advocates [for your brand] – so they are all reaching different channels and [the brand message] is all coming from a person and not a brand [or corporation].

Or would you rather spend your money to slap out your message to reach one million people with a story that's coming from a brand? And so: stop focusing on what's going on with the big numbers. Start focusing on the small numbers that are getting the big returns.

Small numbers, big returns. That's the value of a connected community. That's the value of context.

What is the context that creates exchange for your organization? The Huffington Post has built a community around their business model – and a business model around their community. This organization continues to lead, when it comes to fostering a community...

TIGHTEN THE STORY

How could a new context create new results, for you and your company – through the cultivation of a new kind of community?

Tim McDonald is an example of someone who is taking a leadership role as a community manager, for an iconic worldwide brand.

So the questions for you are:

Who handles your online community?

Who within your organization is identifying and curating content that facilitates exchange?

What are the touch points that you are building, right now, to allow your key audiences to key in on your value proposition?

Sometimes – in fact, many times – that value proposition isn't necessarily about products and services. It's about intelligent discourse to help lead people to valuable decisions. If your product set provides real value, and your community management provides real discourse, you will create real exchange.

Start off by appointing a community manager within your organization. And, if you already have a community manager, start off by appointing thought leaders within key divisions and provide them a new task.

Ask for content creation – blog posts, white papers. Even videos.

Get the folks in R&D, or product management, or shipping involved in sharing what the customers need to know.

Build transparency from inside your organization, by sharing insights from the people within your company. Create an initiative to share new content – organic, internal content – in a way that drives an authentic and value-rich dialogue with the people that matter most. And if you need help finding that dialogue from inside, make sure you hire a consultant that's willing to get inside the hearts and minds of your employees as well as your customers.

Context is king, for your Chief Branding Officer. Make sure that the context comes from the inside, because that's where your most authentic messages live.

Chapter 6: Capitalizing

After all, how do you measure the ROI of a conversation?

RETURN ON RELATIONSHIP BY KATHRYN ROSE
AND TED RUBIN

Conformity is the jailer of freedom and the enemy of growth.

JOHN F. KENNEDY

HOW DO YOU TURN the branding conversation into an asset? How do you take the ideas of listening from Cisco, partner management from Cargill, and community leadership from Huffington Post, and turn it into a tangible result for your organization?

Demographics Are Dead

Since God was a boy, marketers have tried to create effective segmentation strategies in order to provide some sort of ROI (return on investment – an acronym that stands for both justification and job security) on branding efforts.

Demographics – the science of shared characteristics applied to media planning, brand investment and segmentation in an old-school model - looks at who might be most likely to buy a particular product or service. The science of demographics became sophisticated almost instantly, as age groups, income level, education and other data points were built around defining that ever-elusive target market.

Unfortunately, demographic data shares a similar flaw with our higher education system here in the United States. And that's why demographics are dying a slow death.

In an article called "The End of Demographics: How Marketers Are Going Deeper With Personal Data," Mashable author Jamie Beckland says:

> Marketers have built a temple that needs to be torn down. Demographics have defined the target consumer for more than half a century — poorly...The year that someone was born will not

tell you how likely he is to buy your product.[1]

That kind of flawed logic is the same frame of reference that we use in higher education.

The idea that a "college sophomore" is a nineteen-year-old who lives on campus is as outdated as a buggy whip.

Sure, there are sophomores who live on campus, and who are 19 years old.

But there are also sophomores who are:

- Married with two kids, celebrating their 31st birthday
- A 16-year-old prodigy who wants to be a PhD before she's 21
- A 53-year-old grandmother who is taking courses online
- Someone else who breaks the mold by living in a different state, or even a different country, from where the university is located

While their ages and circumstances are wildly divergent, there is something they share in common: their behaviors.

When it's time for class, they are required to attend (go online? tune in to the lecture?) and must act accordingly (or bear the consequences). Assignments are due, for all of these students, at the same time. They have the same professor. You get the idea.

There's a lot of individuality in the modern classroom – the kind of individual characteristics that throw a grenade into the middle of traditional, rigid demographics.

Interestingly enough, our educational system was never intended to foster individuality. But guess what we've got in our classrooms? INDIVIDUALS.

Wouldn't it be great if all people of a certain age behaved the same – especially when it came to consumer behavior?

Wouldn't it be great if organizations of a certain revenue level all behaved the same – especially when it came to purchasing your B2B product?

But we all know that's an uneducated viewpoint.

Interestingly enough, that kind of rigid thinking actually originated in the development of the US educational system.

Our modern education system was developed in 1846.

Based on the Prussian system of learning, the US educational system was designed by Horace Mann to create a uniform method of learning.

(I don't know about you, but I'm suspicious of anything that's described as "modern" that got its start before Lincoln grew a beard).

But Mann wanted a system that could create an assembly-line type of product, and create uniformity in education.

Uniformity. Close cousin to conformity. You've herd of conformity, right? (No, I meant to write "herd." That's not a typo.)

Conformity. Very useful if you want to control an unruly population. Or send out propaganda-like marketing messages, in broad brush strokes, with impressive reach and frequency, to a wide array of eyeballs.

Conformity means "one size fits all," because "all " are the same. Not effective if you want to engage an audience in a real conversation.

Students, regardless of interest or ability, were (and are) ranked based on age. A regimented process (evidenced by rows in the classroom, lecture and rote memorization) was introduced, first by Frederick (that guy was the King of Prussia) and then, through Horace Mann, into the USA.

A strict bureaucracy was built, where the students feared the teacher. The teacher feared the principal, and the principal feared the superintendent.

But don't be afraid: You are probably the product of a similar system, just as am I.

You know all too well the Prussian model. It carried over from elementary school, all the way into my college experience – perhaps yours as well –although new freedoms and flexibilities were introduced. For example, instead of working on redundant math problems, college focused on critical thinking skills. You know, moving towards existential questions like, "Why are we studying calculus?" and "When does happy hour start?"

But, I digress.

The Prussian model was designed to ensure control, efficiency, and effectiveness – much like an ad campaign designed to reach women, ages 25-34, with college educations and household incomes above $85,000 per year.

This idea of a one-size-fits-all, one-path-fits-all, one-speed-fits-all, one-location-fits-all is about as relevant as a screen door on a submarine.

Are you with me?

A branding campaign is a lot like an old word problem from math class.

Do you know the problem? It goes something like this:

> Fred climbs on board a train at Grand Central Station, carrying $5,000 in a briefcase. The train leaves the station at 10:20 am headed for Boston at an average speed of 32 mph. Boston is 224 miles from New York. Assuming the train does not stop and maintains its average speed for the entire journey, at approximately what time will Ted arrive in Boston?

Everyone in math class reads that problem and says, "Who cares?"

But change the wording a little bit, and the problem gets a lot more interesting:

> Fred climbs on board a train at Grand Central Station, carrying *your* $5,000 in a briefcase. The train leaves the station at 10:20 am headed for Boston at an average speed of 32 mph. Boston is

224 miles from New York. Assuming the train does not stop and maintains its average speed, at what time will *your money* arrive in Boston?

The point is: money and train schedules don't really matter – unless they matter to you. The same can be said of your branding.

If you want your story to be relevant, you've got to understand the "Fifth P" in the marketing mix.

Traditional marketing talks about the "four Ps": product, price, promotion and place.

The Fifth P? **Personalization.**

Clients today are looking for resonance – that personalization that makes them feel like your brand is aligned with their values in some personal way. That's especially true for consumer brands and B2C companies. But B2B brands need that connection as well.

While a corporation may not be a person, it certainly has a personality. And that personality is a part of bulletproof branding.

While the details, information and calculations must be important in marketing (otherwise, why go through them?) the most important details are the most personal. At least, to the customer.

Without personalization, your audience isn't involved in your story.

Without personalization, your branding isn't bulletproof. It's disconnected. It's disjointed. It's vulnerable.

The antidote for conformity is individuality. The modern conversation requires individual attention – a compelling aspect of the story that gets your customer involved.

But, how do you know your customer – and how do you know what will get them involved? (Especially since traditional demographics are just not what they used to be).

But market research – and understanding buyer behavior on an individual basis – is alive and well. Unfortunately, so is the Prussian model of education, and dumb word problems in math class, but that's a subject for another book. (Let's focus on one reform at a time).

In order to find out how companies are effectively responding to the need to identify behaviors as well as other data for prediction, I turned to my friend Ben Smithee.[2]

Ben is the managing director of Spych Research, an organization dedicated to helping companies create effective brand strategies – with a keen emphasis on

Generation Y. A Millennial himself, Ben is not only a sought-after speaker but also a recognized thought-leader on how companies can connect most effectively with Gen Y – and across all generations – through greater consumer understanding. Ben is a digital strategist, a television host in the Dallas-Fort Worth area, and an expert at cultivating the conversation for the Millennial generation.

Why is "the conversation" so important to Millennials?

- Because a whopping 48% of Millennials say that word-of-mouth influences their purchases more than TV ads.[3]
- Because "In the new social ecosystem, it's not always the best product/service that wins...it's the best experience that is easiest to share with my friends...," according to Ben

So, how do you create that experience – and make it easy to share – whether your target customer is a Millennial, or a multi-national corporation? I sat down with Ben to gain his insights.

And, in keeping with the spirit of previous chapters (and the key themes of the book) I want to share our conversation, in hopes that it helps to create yours. I've always admired Ben's perspective, and his approach to research has created impressive results for organizations like eBay, General Mills, Coca-Cola, Pfizer and other similar companies around the world.

We actually sat down to consider what you might be able to do, and learn, in order to make sure your branding is absolutely bulletproof. And interestingly enough, Ben starts off by talking about education.

> **Ben Smithee:** It's interesting that we're talking about bulletproof branding, because the customers now have more ammunition than ever. And they're starting to take shots at the brands, and pull the trigger. And they are armed by the environment of social, and by consumer awareness. So, education: for the first time, consumers are as educated about the brand as the brand is educated about their consumers.
>
> Brands have always spent money on consumer intelligence – so, insights and intelligence, which is our game, brands spend a lot of money on that. While consumers have that [same level of insight], but they just look at it via twitter and Wikipedia and blogs and all of the mommy blogs… uncovering what matters to them, whether it's trying to be all-natural with food, or things of that nature.
>
> **CW:** Should brands be scared of social, and the power that's in the hands of the consumer?
>
> **Ben:** If brands don't take the effort to understand [social], then absolutely. Because that brand is

going to screw it up. [Social] creates an opportunity– and it can show their weak spot, as it puts them under a microscope. You can't just preach and market the way that Apple markets. You have to have the culture that Apple has. It's not about the "big name" – it reminds me of what your mom always told you: you have to practice what you preach.

For the first time consumers are really looking at the connection between communication and action, when it comes to brands.

The Age of Conscious Consumerism is here. Everybody says that Gen Y and Boomers "want the same things." The difference is that Millennials are empowered by technology to make decisions and follow up. And put their money where their mouth is. And that's what Millennials are doing. Millennials are taking and calling their own shots; and if a brand isn't armored against those messages they are vulnerable. When we look at brands, we look at it holistically. We don't just evaluate to see if the brand is digitally savvy. We ask: do you have competent sales associates? Do you have competent customer service?

CW: How important is that consistency to Gen Y?

Ben: That consistency is what defines your success.

We live in 140 characters. Our mindset has the attention span of a refresh rate – on Facebook, or in a newsfeed.

So, what is the consumer refresh rate? The consumer refresh rate means that every time the screen refreshes, it's a new opportunity.

A new opportunity to be exposed, a new opportunity to engage, a new opportunity to capitalize on what you can convey. And consistency changes, depending on what you're trying to accomplish with the brand – whether you are in social acquisition versus social conversion versus social equity.

CW: Wait a minute: is this a story about "situational consistency?" That kind of reminds me of situational ethics...

Ben: (*laughs*) Well, there are different aspects of the brand that need to be touted.

"Social acquisition" is how do I capture that feel-good thing? That means the feel-good nature that the conscious consumer is going to look at, from a social perspective. Meaning not "social media," but social and causal in terms of society as a whole - the common good. And "causal" as related and social causes.

Then, social conversion asks how you are doing compared to your competitors. Social conversion takes in new metrics in the measurement of your brand. Pricing is a component of your brand, and a component of acquisition.

Are you trying to gouge the customer or not? Pricing can be all-encompassing [in the eyes of the consumer]. Because consumers don't differentiate, whether you market this way [or that], whether you do this or that, they are judging you based on every single interaction with you.

Today your brand has a lot more "surface area" – you've got a lot more pieces that are exposed to the customer. So, there's a lot more areas of liability – areas where you can screw something up.

CW: Are there any cautionary tales out there of brands that are exposing themselves to unnecessary risk, or unprecedented success, because of this surface area you describe?

Ben: Yeah, look at (eye retailer) Warby Parker. They took on the biggest monopoly out there. When you look at Luxottica…

CW: Yeah, they have like 70% market share…[4]

Ben: Right, so what did Warby Parker say? They said, "You know what? We're going to give you cool frames. We're going to give you – for $95 – frames and lenses. And guess what? If you don't have your prescription, tell us your optometrist's name, and we will call them and get your prescription for you.

"And shipping both ways, with virtual try-on. So, you want to try out five different frames? We'll ship them to you and let you decide, send them back when you make your decision."

They are the Advil of the online shopping process. They take all of the pain away. And it's just – -- that's exactly it. Why would you NOT use them, once you're exposed to them?

And think about when you go to buy glasses: the styles that you have. You look at a style and say, "Oh, if only it were a little bit different." They don't try to have every style out there.

[Warby Parker] has their style, their deal. They took the model, flipped it on its [name of a body part] and said,

"Hey. 95 bucks."

The other aspect of branding is: branding is where content meets commerce. So, before, the quality of the brand was based solely on its value financially...

CW: Isn't that still a valid measure?

Ben: Sure, but the only way you get there is through content.

What's the content of your brand? Not just your blog content or your website content, but the actual content – the "meat" – of your brand.

Where content meets commerce is the definition of your brand.

We are looking at developing a "Spych Scorecard" – defining Millennials' affinity for brands.

Everyone wants to pin branding onto digital, but it's way more than that.

I hate to bust everyone's bubble, but this Gen-Y guy is not going to fall for the "it's all digital" trap.

It is digital, but it's personal.

People still want to have a tangible experience with the brand, still experiential, and people still want to have a connection to the brand.

CW: Is an electronic experience a tangible experience?

Ben: For us [Millennials], it is. It depends on how you define "tangible" but we touch it, we feel it. Do you have to pick up a product? Not necessarily. But what matters is the stickiness, the tangibility of an experience, which can be electronic if it's done correctly.

The trick is to take a physical, tangible thing and make it a digital experience. I mean, look at us: we're here talking, having a conversation about branding and then, all of a sudden, someone takes a picture, posts it online....and you've got the Domino's scandal.[5]

The real-life experiences become digital, and many times those real-life experiences matter even more when they go digital.

As brands are starting to get digital right, they're screwing up the stuff they used to get right.

Take hotels as an example. You've got a noon or 1pm checkout, but you've still got client meetings. So you check out but you've still got some stuff to do before you catch your flight, because you're on business. Some brands charge you to store a bag, so the experience becomes one of being "nickeled and dimed" on your way out the door.

The last thing you want is for the last experience to be one of being nickeled and dimed to store a bag.

You gotta be kidding me.

That's a very tangible personal experience that becomes digital, as soon as I put it out to 3,000 followers, 2500 friends on Facebook. And that connection between my experience and my Twitter account has a direct impact on that hotel brand.

Brands are forgetting that point where worlds collide – between the URL and IRL [in real life]. Both places have tangible experiences. It becomes an interesting spot for the future.

CW: Making digital tangible? Look, aren't we making some demographic generalities about Millennials – not all Millennials are created equal, right?

Ben: Companies are getting better at using online content leading to purchases – leading to store visits. We walked in to Warby Parker in New York – and the store is packed. Old people. Young people. Picking up glasses. Trying them on. But they are still also buying them online.

So, can digital drive retail? Absolutely. The retail experience just has to be compelling enough.

Online, the experience has to give us a feel for that brand, in seven seconds on a mobile website.

You've got seven inches [on a device screen] and seven seconds to watch what's going on - and make a decision on whether I want to follow up any further.

CW: How does the intersection of digital and tangible come together for your clients? Tell me more about Spych and the nature of your business.

Ben: Spych is focused on insights and intelligence. From that standpoint, we're helping brands that want to engage, understand and interact with the Gen Y community. And we're giving them the insights to help them formulate some kind of action. Historically, that's been about asking questions and answering questions. We're focused on taking information and turning it into action [for our clients]. So, we help our customers to understand, "What can we do with this information?" - not just "How much information can we collect?"

Because, from a social media standpoint, a lot of people do "social listening." Well, that's great... but then there's always the question: "So what do we do with these metrics? What do we do with this data?"

What we're looking at is how social insights can lead to actionable intelligence – how do we convert to PR? To marketing? How do we help our customer service or IT department, based on what we're learning from a social media standpoint?

Because of our expertise in social marketing, that's led to an evolution on the other side of our business. That's why we do digital strategy for businesses. A lot of companies have research – they have an abundance of data – but they just now need to know what to do with it.

CW: How do you know what questions to ask when it comes to branding? Are there questions that brands need to be asking, but they're not?

Ben: The problem isn't that big brands ask questions, or ask the wrong questions, and then they listen.

The problem lies in the model. That conversational model doesn't really flow in the right direction.

Brands now have the ability to listen first and then ask strategic questions, instead of sitting there and thinking that, in order to get strategic information from our consumers we have to start asking provocative questions, or asking strategic questions. Or, really, not strategic questions but hypothesized questions – here's a hypothesis, let's ask questions.

Now, we can listen strategically and form some sort of understanding and form a basis for the conversation. That basically flips the conversational model [for branding].

CW: So the conversation starts with listening?

Ben: Yeah. Most conversations start with listening. That's what the consumer does. We sit there and we listen. We sit there and read Amazon reviews. We look at Yelp. We look at TripAdvisor. The consumers are listening before they take action on a brand. They are basically listening to what others say.

A lot of our work focuses on consumers and consumer behavior, but we also have a B2C aspect that's hard for brands to ignore. Here's the basic premise:

All Millennials want a job.

So we also help these businesses to reach a new kind of consumer – a potential hire for the company – by providing them with guidance and best practices for communicating their brand to a market of potential new hires. We help companies to understand how to be a destination employer for Gen Y and Millennials – how to help them work with this generation. What are the things that they desire from an office space setting, for example? As you know, from your expertise, what

[Millennials want] is what everyone wants – just with a different nuance.

And this generation is not afraid to start poking holes – and shooting holes – in a company's branding. Our focus is not just external for the consumers, but internal for the employees. Because, as Millennials become part of the workplace, if you're not branding internally, you're creating exposure from the inside out.

CW: Do you mean a disgruntled employee? [Like the Domino's scandal?]

Ben: If you're a brand, and you stand next to a grenade, that's one thing – but if you're lying on top of a grenade (in other words, if the explosion is coming from within your organization) the damage is going to be a lot worse. You've got to take time to consider an explosion that's led by your employees – that's 100% detrimental. You've got to protect your brand.

CW: While it's true that social media can be a great communicator of truth, it can also be a great place for a bitch session from the nearest loudmouth, or a broadcast mechanism for a terrible video prank. And, sometimes, there's no amount of bulletproof branding that can stop someone - from posting negative messages on YouTube, or Facebook, or wherever.

But, you're really talking about potential employees and job seekers who are listening to the legitimate comments of existing employees, right?

Ben: Think about potential employees as consumers.

Who are these consumers more likely to listen to: others outside of the company, or those on the inside? That one employee that's seen the working inside, and they're yelling and screaming, why wouldn't I listen to what they're saying? Because – if the comments have a ring of truth, and they are not pumping out some prank or raving lunacy – the inside employee has the inside track.

The problem is, companies often look at internal branding as a secondary thing – an afterthought. The truth is, if you're a big company and you get your internal branding right, your employees should be the biggest advocates for your brand. You've got a ton of reach! Every single one of your employees has a family, or friends, a wife, two and a half kids, whatever – what's your brand reach, just from an internal standpoint?

Even if you have 100 employees – as soon as that starts increasing exponentially as they go out and say something positive about your brand? How quickly does that message – at one office - blanket a city?

CW: So, if companies want to expand their reach, the message is: Take care of your people.

Ben: Sure.

How many times have your employees touched and felt the products that you offer?

How many times have they experienced the services you provide?

How many times have they driven your cars, eaten your food, stayed at your hotel?

These are your internal brand monitors. And you could be missing out on that brand equity. Make people happy and you don't have to police them as much. You've got to police a disgruntled employee a lot more than you've got to police a happy one.

Associate "policing employees" with time. Associate that time with cost. Now all of a sudden that cost becomes important, doesn't it? .

TIGHTEN THE STORY

Capitalizing on the power of bulletproof branding begins with your internal employees. Taking care of your people has always been the key to that aspect of your brand. Are you setting clear expectations on how everyone on your payroll – everyone – is a representative of your brand?

Consider this lesson about keeping it personal, from a nursing student. Ann Wilde was in her second month of nursing school when her professor gave her a test. The test seemed fairly easy, but the final question was a bit of a show-stopper:

What is the name of the woman who cleans the school?

The nursing student realized that she had seen the woman many times. But her name was a mystery. She turned in her paper, with a blank on the final question.

A curious student asked the teacher, "Will that final question count towards our grade?"

"Paying attention to the people around you always matters to your grade. And your career."[6]

Turn internal customers into brand advocates, and provide legitimate reasons (and clear instructions) on how employees across all areas of the organization can make a contribution. And recognize the people around you, because *significance* is something that we all share. Who deserves your attention, but isn't receiving it? Who is making a contribution that is going unrecognized? Maybe it is time to make your business more personal.

Krista Kotrla (on twitter @kristakotrla) is Senior Vice President of Marketing at Block Imaging, and she has created a culture of participation for her company that truly leverages and capitalizes on everyone's contribution. She calls it "brand democratization." Here's how she explains why brand democratization matters, on her website, http://kristakotrla.com:

> **It matters to employees.** When you democratize your brand, you are inviting every person in your

organization to make a difference. They aren't just coming to work to collect a paycheck and do a job. They're there to do meaningful work. Inspired employees are more likely to contribute innovative ideas, embrace change and build a community of collaboration.

It matters to consumers. When you democratize your brand, you are inviting every person who shares your mission and values to do more than make a purchase. You're inviting them to participate in something important. You're also inviting them to be advocates, amplify the mission and make an impact in their own spheres of influence.

It matters to be a more human brand. When you democratize your brand, it becomes alive, more human, more authentic because of the people representing it. Your brand becomes so much more than a logo and a few sound bites dreamed up by the marketing department. Your brand has heart. It has stories. It has enduring relationships. It has a commitment to something bigger.

It matters to the community. When you democratize your brand, you are confirming for employees and consumers, "You matter. Let's achieve something great together." And what you can be achieve together is much more powerful than what any one person alone can achieve.

How could your organization harness the power of a democratized brand? Could your company build and create blog posts from internal employees – talking about what it's really like to engineer your electronics products, work within the supply chain for Johnson & Johnson, or deliver high-quality cancer treatments at your clinic?

The trusted voice of the democratized brand is the voice of the internal employee.

Your potential customers and future employees are listening. And they are curious to learn more.

Do your employees have a voice, and a venue, to share the story of your brand?

Chapter 7: Craving

The starting point of all achievement is desire.

NAPOLEON HILL

WHAT TURNS A CUSTOMER into a raving, craving brand advocate?

In the age of momentary loyalty and shifting alliances, that connection with your Chief Branding Officer is the key to bulletproof branding. But where does that impulse to share, guide and advise come from? The experience you've had. Think about this for a second;

Consumed by the new economy, and lack of consumer interest, all products and services have all been replaced by what we now call "Experiences."

Calling something a product or service just doesn't make

any sense in the new economy. The description is out of date, the words don't apply to today's *branding*.

Marketers and sales people need to understand:

> *You are no longer selling and marketing products and services. You are selling and marketing experiences.*

We buy, acquire, endure and enjoy experiences. Not products. Not services. Experiences.

Welcome to the new economy, where commerce trades on the experience you have, and the experience you provide.

Consider these experiential products:

- A vacation in Hawai'i
- A new app for your iPhone
- Purchasing a new Nissan Altima
- Attending a play, museum or movie
- Transitioning to SAP CRM

Which of these are products, and which are services? Answer: None, and all. The old words don't work anymore; we need to choose new ones if we want to tell a story that's authentic and complete. And all customers – all consumers – *crave authenticity*.

You see, no product exists in a vacuum. No service stands alone without products. These things are really events, or **experiences**, made up of a series of products, services and interactions.

What we want, what we pay for and what we get can all be summed up in one way: experiences.

Even a traditional product purchase, like buying a new car, requires a series of events that create an experience that circumvents the "product."

For example, when you buy a car, unless you have $48,433.00 cash (hey, that's a pretty nice car! But, of course, if you are reading this book I know you appreciate the finer things in life), you are going to need financing. Maybe you will lease the vehicle. Maybe you will talk to the finance manager, or the sales manager, about your options.

You go through a series of events and choices; this is all part of the experience of ownership. The most traditional "product" in America (the automobile) gives you an experience. The experience of the purchase, the experience of the service, and the experience of the *brand*.

How does your car make you feel about yourself? Are you comfortable, and do you feel powerful behind the wheel? Those feelings are as real as the tires and the spark plugs – a very real *brand experience*, indeed.

Our impulse to connect is based on a psychological need that we all share. Why?

Because we all want to share our experiences! (That's the classic answer to the question, "Why does Facebook exist?" and probably the follow-up, "Why is Facebook being replaced?" – but that's a subject for another book!)

Ask yourself this question:

Do you share information – either in person or online – in order to help people to see you as:

- Intelligent?
- Resourceful?
- Clever?
- Funny?
- Savvy and "in-the-know" about particular issues or trends?

Your intentions – everyone's intentions – aren't just designed to impress. Social sharing is at the core of what makes us human. Mankind's ability to share and connect is the reason we sit at the top of the food chain. Our communication skills and connectivity separate us from a world of stronger, larger and more dangerous beasts, able to build buildings and launch metal tubes into space. Among other things.

So why wouldn't you want to use your super-human superpowers for the common good?

If your review of a product helps someone to make a wise decision (or avoid a huge mistake), why wouldn't you offer it?

The conversation online is based on the model of sharing – a model that dates from the mid-90s, and the advent of the commercial Internet.

Our sense of belonging is a highly developed intrinsic motivator. That belonging leads us to brands like American Express – where membership has its privileges – or to any number of other groups. Whether consumer or corporate, associations are all around us. Some of these associations may connect us professionally – to other attorneys, chefs or hairdressers – or to friends who share a common interest in vampire novels, field hockey or the Tony awards.

Groups exist for every possible interest and profession, as humans are social creatures. And consider your own socialization for a second, when you consider the greatest living punishment in the world.

Imagine a prison, filled with the worst hardened criminals. These criminals are already separated from society – set apart – as part of their punishment.

Yet, inside the walls of the prison, when criminals misbehave, what happens?

Solitary confinement.

If isolation is our greatest punishment, social connection is our greatest gift – our greatest asset.

What brands have to understand is that sharing is our norm – not the exception.

Creating a craving among your customers – and turning your clients into advocates – means providing two things:

- A great solution for your clientele
- A great way for your clientele to share their experiences with others

Why isolate your customers from your branding by ignoring their tweets, and leaving their comments alone?

What message does that send, regarding the conversation?

In a recent coaching session, my client was perplexed. And she asked me a question that I hadn't anticipated.

Just coming off of a three-day corporate sales training, she had been taught the importance of "features and benefits" in the sales process. Like most traditional sales training, she had experienced one of the three most common outcomes (first is boredom, second is confusion, third is a search for relevance). She was engaged with the training, but confused by the concept of features and benefits. I can certainly understand the confusion around these two most-fundamental concepts. Because I understand the confusion, and try to focus on what's relevant, I never talk about features and benefits with my clients. Ever.

That's why coaching is more focused than training – it avoids the unnecessary and concentrates on your goals and objectives. Because, if you don't need the material in chapter 3, there's no need to discuss it. Unless, today you are in a class. And the syllabus says, "Chapter 3."

Welcome to Ineffectiveness 101.

But today we were not in a lock-step training program. We weren't about worried grades or certificates. We were concentrating on results.

Talking about features and benefits is like teaching a graduate student about basic multiplication. With a textbook from 1968.

Redundant? Perhaps. And outdated.

I try to focus on more powerful ideas, like "solutions" and "outcomes" in the sales process. But, if you've ever carried a bag (or managed people who do) you understand that there is a very practical and tactical aspect of sales.

It has been said that sales is where the rubber meets the road. And marketing is where the rubber meets the sky.

Bulletproof branding is where marketing and sales meet each other for the first time, jump in the car and head down the road together, while singing along to the same song on the radio.

Look, don't get me wrong: features and benefits are important. They are fundamental, in many ways.

But features and benefits don't really apply to modern sales and marketing strategy.

My client explains why: In her three-day sales training, she was told that it was important to sell the benefits, not the features.

She believed (rightly so) that, when she was meeting with customers, she was focused solely on the features (what the product does). Working with software, at a technology company, the distinction of features from benefits was difficult - because the benefit IS what the product does, in many cases.

Her confusion took the form of a straightforward question. Maybe it's a question you've asked yourself, but never had the courage to voice it out loud. Here it is:

> *I'm not sure what the difference is between features and benefits.*

And, if you are certain you know the difference, be prepared for a new (and challenging) thought. Are you ready?

The reason it is difficult to distinguish features from benefits is:

The person who decides if something is a feature or a benefit isn't you.

It's your customer.

Take a moment to reflect on the role of the customer in the features/benefits conversation.

Let's say you've identified a benefit of your product.

In simple terms, let's just say that your product is faster. I don't know what it does exactly, but it does it faster.

The benefit to your customer is time savings, greater efficiency, and higher productivity.

Right?

Wrong.

If and only if the customer agrees that higher productivity, time savings and greater efficiency are important can those so-called benefits become real and tangible benefits.

Now, hold on - you may be thinking - everyone wants greater efficiency, higher productivity and time savings! Those elements are benefits - those words describe the outcomes and results of certain features, applied in action! You're way off base here! Those are not benefits, they are FEATURES!

Look, I don't disagree with you. Or your reasoning. The all caps thing is a little much, Gunga Din, but I hear you loud and clear.

But my opinion about benefits doesn't really matter.

And neither does yours.

The person who decides what "benefits" are isn't you, or me. It's your customer.

If You Say:	Your Customer Hears:
"It's a Benefit"	"It's a Feature"

If Your Customer Says:	Then You Hear:
"It's a Benefit"	The Truth.

As I explained this to my coaching client, she realized that the only way to identify benefits is by getting buy-in and agreement from the customer.

Because, if you think time savings, greater efficiency, and higher productivity are important to every customer out there...well, you've never sold to state and local government.

If you want to find the true benefits, you have to ask an expert. And that expert isn't you or me. It's your customer.

> *Nativo CMO Jason Choi said that the #1 mistake marketers make with branded content is "approaching [branded content] from the brand's point of view."*[1]

The point is, what you believe to be true about your brand is important. But what your customer believes about your brand is what makes it bulletproof.

As you create your brand message, don't guess about benefits. Don't project wants, needs and solutions, as Jason Choi suggests. Create a dialogue - and that dialogue can be fostered via a variety of channels.

Let's face it. Sales isn't so much about what you do... It's about what your customer does. When the order is placed, sales happens. Benefits are identified in a way that creates exchange.

Oh, and if the mention of "sales" makes you roll your eyes and wish you were reading Seth Godin's blog, please don't. (Not that Seth doesn't have great material!)

It's a fact that sales is an aspect of marketing, and vice versa.

Because branding isn't a part of your business. It is your business.

The presentation, PowerPoints, lunches and phone calls are all part of the sales process. So are the logo, and the advertising, pricing and the publicity.

But confirmation - and action - is where the sale takes place.

What if selling something isn't so much about broadcasting features, benefits and solutions? What if sales is really about teaching the customer how to buy?

Stop selling. Start teaching the customer how to buy.

What if your sales force plugged in that simple idea: what would change for your brand? For your business?

Consider:

- **Get Into the Education Business, Today:** Teach the customer how to buy. Build a plan, today, around re-shaping your "sales" team into something that everyone wants and needs. No one wants to be "sold." But everyone wants to buy. Create a team of teachers, who facilitate exchange

- the exchange of ideas for goods and services. If that philosophy describes your sales team, you are getting more and more bulletproof by the minute!

- **Social, Seriously:** Selling today - just like branding and all phases of business - is more social than ever. The line between sales and marketing – not unlike the line between work/life balance – is blurred. (That whole work/life thing? I think it's just "life." The distinction is just wishful thinking, and not necessarily accurate. The same can be said of sales and marketing – both need to be a part of the same exchange, wouldn't you agree?)

The proliferation of information and content on the Internet means that your sales team (and your marketing team – how about just your entire business team?) faces the same challenge as your customer: How do we sort through the bazillions of bytes of data, to find the story that's relevant? Beyond the answers that Google and Bing provide, consider how your branding has to help curate the content that's already out there. Telling clients and customers how to do something can be important; but showing them where to look, teaching them the information that matters, and guiding them simply through a complex process is much more than just "important." Guiding customers through a conversation towards the messages that matter is empowering. Your action is to guide, direct, listen and empower.

- **Get Different:** What's the difference between encouragement, and empowerment? A lot of companies talk about "empowerment" but what they're really describing is encouragement. There's an important distinction between these two concepts.

  - *Encouragement* provides the confidence you need to move forward; encouragement is made up of positive reinforcement and guidance on the next steps. Encouragement makes you feel good, and should inspire you to take action.

  - *Empowerment* takes encouragement one step further. If you are empowered, you feel good about your next move...and you have the tools to make it happen. Empowerment involves a process. In order to move from encouragement to empowerment, you have to have tools and steps for your next action or series of actions.

Encouragement inspires confidence; empowerment inspires a clear set of steps and actions designed to create a result. And, those steps are supported by tools or processes, to generate the desired outcome. So, if your team doesn't have clear steps, effective tools, and the ability to take action, you will need to give them lots of encouragement instead.

But unfortunately, encouragement doesn't feed the bulldog.

Encouragement isn't enough to create exchange.

Feeling good about your past performance, and feeling clear about what you need to do next, doesn't mean you can do it.

Branding becomes vulnerable when team members don't have the tools to take action.

When people know what to do, and how to do it, that's empowerment.

And, if they don't take the required action, that's cause for a different kind of conversation.

But, if you are a business leader, don't take "empowerment" lightly. Encourage wherever you can, to inspire the results you need. An inspired organization will carry that inspiration to the customers, and to every facet of the business.

But an empowered organization runs on more than just confidence and good feelings. An empowered organization has the tools and the processes to take the conversation to the next level.

What tools are in place to empower your company, your message, and your brand? And following our theme of "ask the customer if you want to identify the benefits," you might want to ask your team members if they agree to your assessment of empowerment. I'd like to encourage you in that regard!

- **Get to the Customer:** What if teaching the customer how to buy was a part of every facet of your organization?

    o How would that approach change the dynamic within your teams, and your ability to execute in a way that takes "cross-functional" from a concept into a competitive advantage?

    o Only a cohesive company is bulletproof. What is the internal message or theme that unifies your organization?

- **Get the Benefits:** Benefits are what the customer sees, not you. Confirmation is required for any benefit. Otherwise, it's still a feature. The message is delivered differently, whether from marketing or sales. But that message has to be cohesive. And that message has to be confirmed by the customer.

- **Get Going:** Action is needed to confirm the features. What action does your branding inspire from your customers?

    Traditional marketing focuses on the "call to action" as if it's a thing within your website, your collateral, your ad campaign.

    The call to action isn't a single thing - it's everything.

    If you aren't moving the conversation forward, you're not creating exchange.

If your message does create exchange, you are creating an exchange of thoughts and ideas (that's a call to action), an exchange of information in return for greater engagement (that's a call to action) and ultimately an exchange of products and services for money (also a call to action).

Inspire and empower action from your customer at every possible opportunity - that's what engagement is really all about. Create the conversation and watch closely for the actions that confirm that your branding is bulletproof.

- **Get Referrals:** Speaking of conversation, and empowerment: How are you creating the conversation around the benefits of your product? What tools - online and in person - are in place, right now, for your branding? What tools should be in place? (More on those questions in future chapters)

- **Get Connected to Your Sales Team:** How are you incorporating feedback from your sales team into your marketing?

I know... The reason you studied marketing in college is so that you wouldn't have to work in sales.

But, let's face it. Revenues are the reason for the enterprise. If marketing is a silo, and sales is an island, your branding isn't bulletproof.

Is there a bridge between marketing and sales? There should be.

Branding is your business. But still:

Silos are simple, and silos are comforting.

The problem is, no one in a silo knows or cares about what's going on outside.

The silo kills conversation - unless you enjoy talking to yourself.

Gazing into a mirror of marketing, or sales, or even engineering is not helping to make your organization bulletproof.

Where's the Chief Branding Officer in your silo?

The Chief Branding Officer wants (and deserves) a cohesive connection from all the resources within the company. Connections are the key to customer satisfaction, and those connections have to exist within the organization as well.

In the traditional marketing world, you can conduct focus groups – if your budget and brand supports that kind of input.

However, if your budget is more modest, there's still a way to connect with the customer's perceived benefits. Those methods include:

- Surveys, as in SurveyMonkey and other free online tools
- Reviewing comments on Facebook, blog posts, twitter and social media
- Coaching your sales team to ask for confirmation on every "benefit," by using a variation of this simple phrase:

- ○ "How does [that benefit I just threw out there] fit for your organization?"
- ○ "Would you agree that [the benefit I just threw out there] would benefit you?"

Then, whether online or in person, your next step is both incredibly difficult and deceptively simple at the same time:

You have to listen. .

TIGHTEN THE STORY

'What if' unlocks the key to imagination.

STANISLAVSKY

When you are talking to your boss, your team, your investors or your entire organization, consider these seven words as your personal connection point:

"What would it mean to you if…"

Have you stopped to consider what your brand really means to your customers, your employees, or even your investors?

Have you listened, learned and dove deeper into what your solutions really mean?

If you are speaking one-on-one in a persuasive context, you must sincerely ask this question.

The ellipsis (also called "three dots in a row," where I'm from) is there for you to fill in the blanks around the subject at hand. Maybe it's a proposal for a new warehouse in Dutchess County. Or an initiative that targets British Columbia. Or a great idea for sushi on Friday night.

Don't just imagine that you have value to your clients.

Get clear on how you win.

Why do people choose you, over the myriad of alternatives out there? For your non-profit organization, ask yourself why people donate their time and money to you, instead of elsewhere.

And, most importantly, ask them.

Sincerely and clearly asking that question – and listening closely to the response – will make sure your conversation never gets off track.

Before you move on to slide 97, get clear on your vision – and get clear on what it means to your listener.

Transform the conversation in seven words – *"What would it mean to you if…"*

That's all it takes!

Conclusions

IS THE BRANDING CONVERSATION ever really concluded?

The idea of *BulletProof Branding* is to create an ongoing dialogue – for yourself, for your company and for your customers. That dialogue is the genesis of exchange.

The exchange you want to create begins with your story. And sometimes a good storyteller listens first, so that the context for the story is exactly right.

Over these chapters, you've seen how multi-national companies and individuals address some of the specific branding challenges within their organizations. But none of their stories are as important as yours.

By providing examples and best practices, you've seen how the marketplace conversation has changed. But the goal of this book is action. In other words, enabling you to be aware of new strategies, and new tactics, that can help you to change the conversation.

When my wife and I had just gotten married, before we had any kids or anything like that, she went out to a thrift store to do some shopping.

I was in graduate school at the time, and we didn't have much money, and she was doing what she does best: looking for deals.

And she saw this scarf in the thrift store.

A scarf.

And on the scarf was a beautiful picture of a castle, and underneath the castle was a picture of a golden, flowing ribbon. On the ribbon were the words, "Romeo and Juliet."

And my wife saw this scarf, and thought to herself, "I wonder if my husband and I will ever have a daughter.

"And if we do, I wonder if she will ever grow up to play Juliet one day?

"I'll buy this scarf."

And she bought it. It probably cost less than two dollars. And she kept it across the years (because she's a bit of a pack rat, but that's another story).

And on the night that my oldest daughter stepped on stage to play Juliet in a local production of *Romeo and Juliet*, we knew exactly what to give her for an opening night gift.

From that humble thrift store, many years ago, a simple thought for my wife had turned into an unforgettable memory for my entire family.

On that night, I learned that the actions you take, no matter how small, can make a big difference. You can create events and opportunities that may be outside of your wildest imagination right now, if you simply take action.

For you and for your business, don't miss the opportunity that's right in front of you. Take the action you need to build the results you want. Your next step might be something simple – something far-fetched – something creative – something collaborative.

That action begins with your story – the story you tell yourself, and the story you tell your customers. That story can create results beyond your imagination, if you take the time to build the right kind of conversation.

I want to thank you for sharing in my story, and I hope it helps you to tell yours. Because when your conversation is strong, your brand is truly bulletproof.

Acknowledgements

THIS BOOK NEVER WOULD have been possible without the support of people I truly respect. To Jeffrey Hayzlett, a friend and mentor, I thank you for helping me to think big. To Kelly Marc Alston, who is in charge of keeping a tent over my circus, I sincerely appreciate your constant input and enthusiasm. To Tara Alemany, thank you for your reviews and assistance. And to all the audience members who have heard me speak, all the Vistage members who have helped me to hone this content, and to all my contributors, I thank you from the bottom of my heart. And to my friend, Michael Neill, for your subtle yet powerful influence – thank you, sir, for always making a difference.

To Karen Mangia, Mike Fernandez, Ben Smithee, Katy Kiem, Krista Kotrla and everyone else who shared their vision so that this book could come to life, I sincerely appreciate everything you've done to help further the branding conversation.

Finally, and most importantly, to my family: my beautiful wife, Lisa-Gabrielle Greene, and our two daughters: I thank you for your patience, your support and your love during this process. And, I'm very glad to know that our story goes on!

- CW

Endnotes

Introduction

1. "Broken Guitar Has United Playing the Blues to the Tune of $180 Million," July 30, 2009, http://www.fastcompany.com/1320152/broken-guitar-has-united-playing-blues-tune-180-million.

2. "Real Madrid Tops the World's Most Valuable Sports Teams," July 15, 2013, http://www.forbes.com/sites/kurtbadenhausen/2013/07/15/real-madrid-tops-the-worlds-most-valuable-sports-teams/.

3. "Chipotle Faked Its Twitter Hack," July 24, 2013, http://mashable.com/2013/07/24/chipotle-faked-twitter-hack/.

4. YouTube Statistics, last accessed March 4, 2014, http://www.youtube.com/yt/press/statistics.html.

5. "TV is Dying, and Here Are the Stats that Prove It," November 24, 2013, http://www.businessinsider.com/cord-cutters-and-the-death-of-tv-2013-11.

6. "Facebook and Google are about to Overtake all of TV in Audience Size," November 2013, http://www.businessinsider.com/facebook-and-google-to-overtake-tv-in-reach-2013-11.

7. "Britons Spend One in 12 Waking Minutes Online, Pushing Ad Spend to Record High," October 7, 2013, http://www.theguardian.com/media/2013/oct/07/btitons-online-ad-spemd.

8. "$4M for Super Bowl Ad? Guess Who's Buying?" December 4, 2013, http://www.usatoday.com/story/money/business/2013/12/04/super-bowl-advertising-marketing-fox-commercials/3862761/.

Chapter 4

1. The year Cargill was founded.

2. "NGO" stands for Non-Governmental Organization – these are legal institutions that operate independently from any form of government. Typically these organizations have social goals with potential political implications, but they are not openly political. According to Wikipedia, there are over 1 million NGOs in the US.

3. MacMillan salvaged Cargill from the brink of bankruptcy via a major bank restructuring, just prior to World War I.

4. The third largest state in Brazil and an area of exceptional agricultural production.

5. Professor emeritus at the University of Maryland, considered by many to be the top global expert on PR theory.

Chapter 5

1. "Top 10 Most Popular Political Websites - 2013," November 29, 2013, http://www.politisite.com/2013/11/29/top-10-most-popular-political-websites-2013/.

2. Find out more about Tim McDonald by following him on Twitter @tamcdonald. And see what all the fuss is about at http://live.huffingtonpost.com.

Chapter 6

1. "The End of Demographics: How Marketers are Going Deeper with Personal Data," June 30, 2011, http://mashable.com/2011/06/30/psychographics-marketing/.

2. Find out more about Ben Smithee online at http://www.linkedin.com/in/benjaminsmithee or on twitter @SpychResearch.

3. http://www.slideshare.net/bwsmithee

4. Actually, it's north of 80%, as of this writing. Luxottica owns the top eyewear brand worldwide, Ray-Ban, and has over 7,000 stores in the USA alone. Find out more on the Luxottica brand from Forbes Magazine author Dean Crutchfield, http://onforb.es/IRiChV.

5. In 2009, a couple of Domino's employees created a video prank – placing a narrated video on YouTube of a Domino's employee doing some disgusting things

in the preparation of Domino's products. The video quickly reached viral status – viewed over one million times – resulting in felony charges, terminations for the employees... and millions of nauseated viewers. Read the full story on the New York Times website, http://nyti.ms/1biS0PW.

6. "Would You Pass the Dorothy Test?" December 5, 2008, http://community.businessballs.com/blogs/would-you-pass-the-dorothy-test-.html.

Chapter 7

1. "The CMO.com Interview: Nativo CEO Justin Choi," July 18, 2013, http://www.cmo.com/articles/2013/7/18/nativo_cmocom_interview.html.

Contact Info

For more information on how you can put these ideas into action for your organization, contact

WESTFALL AND ASSOCIATES LLC

Interactive workshops | Keynotes | Seminars

5760 Legacy Drive
Suite B3-454
Plano, TX 75024

http://westfallonline.com

214-205-4662